EPITAPHS

EPITAPHS

Graveyard Humour & Eulogy

Compiled by

W. H. BEABLE

NEW YORK

THOMAS Y. CROWELL COMPANY

Publishers

Republished by Singing Tree Press, Book Tower, Detroit, 1971

Library of Congress Catalog Card Number 79-154494

TO THE
HON. JOHN RELLSTAB
JUDGE OF THE U.S. DISTRICT COURT OF
NEW JERSEY, IN MEMORY OF
FORTY YEARS' UNBROKEN
FRIENDSHIP

PREFACE

CONSIDERING the great interest taken in epitaphs, an interest that is shown by numerous articles from time to time in the Press, it is somewhat surprising that no general collection of British epitaphs has been published for many years. In past centuries the works of Weever, Stowe, Pettigrew and others, as well as occasional contributions on the subject by Dr. Johnson and other writers, as introductions to antiquarian and cognate articles, gave expression to, and met the demands of, the public interest in these memorials of the past. But these books, and even the more recent ones, have not only long since been out of print, but have also almost entirely disappeared from any other than the largest reference libraries, and are inaccessible to the general public. They were, moreover, written more for the student and the antiquarian than for popular reading.

If, therefore, this collection does not exactly " fill a long-felt want," it may at least prove of interest to many readers. I have drawn freely from the published examples of the writers referred to, from old books, magazines and periodicals, and from graveyards and other sources, while I am further indebted to many correspondents in all parts of the country for local specimens of obituary effusions.

That so many epitaphs should, in spite of the gravity of the subject, find expression in humorous and even ludicrous verse, is somewhat extraordinary, but it has always been recognised that any collection of epitaphs must partake to a large extent, of a humorous character.

I have not attempted to make the largest collection possible. This book, however, contains many epitaphs not previously published, and is thoroughly representative, including British monumental inscriptions from the earliest period to the present time and of every type and character.

A large number of epitaphs have been omitted for want of space, and these may, perhaps, be published later in another volume, to which I invite contributions from my readers.

WM. HY. BEABLE.

58, Kirkstall Road,
    Streatham Hill, S.W.
        April, 1925.

CONTENTS

ABOUT EPITAPHS

ABOUT EPITAPHS

" Let's talk of graves of worms and epitaphs."—SHAKESPEARE.

> The hills
> Rock-ribbed and ancient as the sun ; the vales
> Stretching in pensive quietness between ;
> The venerable woods ; rivers that move
> In majesty, and the complaining brooks
> That make the meadows green ; and poured round all
> Old ocean's gray and melancholy waste
> Are but the solemn decorations all
> Of the great tomb of man.

MORE than two hundred generations of mortal men lie buried in this vast cemetery of land and ocean that we call the earth.   Mountain and forest, jungle and steppe, and even the billows of the ocean are nature's adornment of the habitations of the dead.   Man has in every age set up memorials to those that " slumber in its bosom."   Church-yards, cemeteries, pyramids, funeral galleries cut into rocks, catacombs, mounds, barrows all abound in every part.

The meditation of the tombs has inspired our great philosophers, poets and writers in all ages.   Dante and Shakespeare found in the graveyard the inspiration for their greatest genius and some of the sublimest thoughts of more modern poets have been associated with the graveyard and the tomb.

The study of epitaphs not only affords a panorama of moral and intellectual expression through the centuries, it is the historian's fundamental guide to the story of the past.   The funereal tablets of Persia, the pyramids and obelisks of Egypt, the monuments of Greece and the catacombs of Rome have unveiled the hidden mysteries

3

of long past centuries and dynasties. The antiquarian makes his researches amid the "tombs of the Kings" and reveals the ancient splendours of past ages.

In our own country, the monumental inscriptions on brass and stone, confined at first to the illustrious and great, contribute to the veneration in which we hold our venerable abbeys, cathedrals, minsters, and our ancient churches, and also have unique historical value. Nearly all our leading poets from Ben Jonson to Wordsworth have found some of their happiest expression in epitaphal eulogy.

As to what constitutes, or should constitute an epitaph, there is considerable divergence of opinion.

Weever, whose "Funeral Monuments," published three hundred years ago, is the first work on epitaphs in the English language, defines an epitaph as "a superscription either in verse or prose ; or an astrict pithy diagram, written, carved, or engraven upon the tomb, grave or sepulchre of the defunct, briefly declaring, (and that, sometimes, with a kind of commiseration) the name, the age, the deserts, the dignitaries, the state, the praises both of body and mind, the good or bad fortunes in life, and the manner and time of the death of the person therein interred."

Sir William Dethick, Garter King of Arms, would have them confined, as was the ancient custom, to those eminent in public service or distinguished by extraordinary virtues and talents. He describes epitaphs as "inscriptions of writings, or the forms of ensigns, motts, or remembrances, engraved or fixed upon sepulchres, tombs or monuments, where the bodies of valiant and most worthy men have been buried."

Puttenham in the "Art of English Poesie" says that "an epitaph is but a kind of epigram only applied to the report of the dead person's estate and degree, or of his other good or bad partes, to his commendation or reproach : and is an inscription such as a man may commodiously write or engrave upon a tombe in few verses, pithie, quicke

and sententious, for the passer-by to peruse and judge
upon without any long tariaunce : so as if it exceede the
measure of an epigram, it is then (if the verse be corre-
spondent) rather an elegy than an epitaph, which errour
many of these bastarde rimers commit, because they be
not learned, for they make long and tedious discourses,
and write them in large tables to be hanged up in churches
and chauncells over the tombes of great men and others,
which be so exceeding long as one must have halfe a daye's
leisure to reade one of them, and must be called away
before he come halfe to the end, or else be locked into the
church by the sexton, as I myself was once served reading
an epitaph in a certain cathedrall church of England.
They be ignorant of poesie that call such long tales by the
name of epitaphes ; they might better call them elegies,
as I said before, and these ought neither to be engraven
nor hanged up in tables. I have seene them, nevertheless,
upon many honourable tombes of those late times erected,
which doe rather disgrace than honour either the writer
or maker."

Dr. Johnson, according to Boswell, considered that
" the writer of an epitaph should not be considered as
saying nothing but what is strictly true ; but that allowance
must be made for some degree of exaggerated praise. In
lapidary inscriptions a man is not upon his oath." The
doctor was also of the opinion that an epitaph should be
" an inscription engraven on a tomb *in honour* of the person
deceased."

Dr. Pettigrew, whose " Chronicle of the Tombs "
published about 70 years ago, is the latest critical contribution on the subject says " there are no specific rules
to determine the formation of epitaphs, either with regard
to their construction or as respects their contents, or the
manner in which these shall be stated ; it is, however,
universally admitted that terseness of expression is an
essential requisite. They may recount the virtues and
glorious actions of the deceased, and hold them up for
our imitation ; and they may also narrate the descent

of the individual, and may mourn his loss. A moral or admonitory precept, too, may be conveyed. An epitaph should unquestionably be brief, and should combine beauty of expression with tenderness of feeling. All that is expressive of love, sorrow, faith, hope, resignation, and piety, should characterise an epitaph. It ought to be made almost exclusively applicable to the individual interred, and certainly not too long for remembrance. Its object is to record what is worthy of remembrance, and to excite sympathy in the beholder. True and genuine sorrow is never loquacious. In conveying consolation and admonition, it should have reference to the common lot of all, and teach us to look up from the grave to a higher sphere of existence."

Fuller, in his usual quaint style, speaking of epitaphs, says : " The shortest, plainest, and truest are the best. I say the shortest ; for when a passenger sees a chronicle written on a tomb, he takes it on trust some great man is there buried, without taking pains to examine who he is. I say also the plainest, for except the sense lie above ground, few will trouble themselves to dig for it."

Mr. W. Browning Smith expresses the opinion that while epitaph etymologically means strictly an inscription upon a tomb, " by a natural extension of usage the name is applied to anything written ostensibly for that purpose whether actually inscribed upon a tomb or not. The most obvious external condition that suitability for mural inscription imposes is one of right limitation as to length. An inscription cannot in the nature of things extend to the proportions that may be required in an elegy."

It is certain that actual inscriptions on tombstones vary considerably from all these definitions, as the examples given in this book will show. There are some as denunciatory as most are eulogistic. There are a few that for beauty of poetical expression are unsurpassed in the English language and others that are as absurd and ludicrous as could be imagined. Most are highly reverential, but many are, intentionally or otherwise, decidedly humorous.

Anagrams, acrostics and puns on names are quite frequent and often combined with lofty sentiment that ignores any incongruity. Kings and heroes, statesmen and warriors, poets and philosophers, receive their due meed of eulogy and sometimes denunciation; husbands set forth the merits and demerits of their deceased spouses, who equally express their opinions of the virtues or otherwise of their former partners. There are epitaphs we would choose for those we know; epitaphs we would perhaps like to have inscribed on our own tombstones.

The earlier British epitaphs were almost entirely in Latin engraved on brass tablets and were usually confined to a statement of the name and rank of the deceased, preceded by the words " Hic jacet." They were, moreover, largely confined to those commemorative of Kings and Princes. In the 13th century French began to be used in writing epitaphs and most of the inscriptions to historical personages about that time are in that language and generally conclude with an urgent request for prayers for the departed.

It was not until the time of Elizabeth that inscriptions were generally written in English and the brass tablet was superseded by the stone monument. They, moreover, assumed a distinct literary character and that on the Dowager Countess of Pembroke, attributed to Ben Jonson and given on another page, is one of the best known and most largely quoted in the language. By a natural extension of use the term epitaph also came to be applied to anything written ostensibly for that purpose whether actually inscribed on a tomb or not, and many of the best known epitaphs are merely literary memorials and find no place on sepulchral monuments.

Such is one of the finest epitaphs in the English language, that by Milton on Shakespeare.

" What needs my Shakespeare, for his honoured bones,
The labour of an age in piled stones ?
Or that his hallowed reliques should be hid

B

Under a star-pointing pyramid ?
Dear Son of Memory, great heir of fame,
What need'st thou such weak witness of thy name ?
Now in our wonder and astonishment
Hast built thyself a life-long monument.
For whilst, to the shame of slow-sounding art,
Thy easy numbers flow ; and that each heart
Hath, from the leaves of thy unvalued book,
Those Delphic lines with deep impression took ;
Then thou our fancy of itself bereaving,
Doth make us marble with too much conceiving ;
And so sepulchred, in such pomp dost he
That kings for such a tomb would wish to die."

And another that by Pope on Sir Isaac Newton :

> " Nature and Nature's laws lay hid in night :
> God said, Let Newton be ! and all was light."

Pope, however, wrote several epitaphs that were actually inscribed on tombstones, the most famous being that on Mrs. Corbet given among the " Ancient Epitaphs " in this volume.

Dr Johnson also wrote some very beautiful English epitaphs, the following example being on Phillips, a musician :—

> " Phillips, whose touch harmonious could remove
> The pangs of guilty power or hapless love :
> Rest here, distressed of poverty no more,
> Here find that calm thou gav'st so oft before :
> Sleep undisturbed within this peaceful shrine
> Till angels wake thee with a note like thine ! "

Ben Jonson was a prodigy of learning and literary energy. And he lived the strenuous London life, going everywhere and meeting everyone of note. He was the friend of Drayton, Donne and Chapman ; he was intimate at times with Bacon ; and he was the loved " master " of a band

of young poets which included Herrick and Suckling.
Also he was the welcome guest of several noble families—
the Sidneys, the Earl of Pembroke, and the Duke and
Duchess of Newcastle. It was as a friend, and not merely
as a courtly poet, that he wrote what is perhaps the most
superb epitaph in the language, though it is also ascribed
to Wm. Browne :—

> " Underneath this sable hearse
> Lies the subject of all verse,
> Sidney's sister, Pembroke's mother :
> Death ! ere thou hast slain another
> Learn'd, and fair, and good as she
> Time shall throw a dart at thee.
>
> Marble piles let no man raise
> To her name for after days ;
> Some kind woman born as she,
> Reading this, like Niobe
> Shall turn mourner, and become
> Both her mourner and her tomb."

Benjamin Franklin devised this quaint conceit for his
own tombstone :—

The Body
of
BENJAMIN FRANKLIN
printer
(like the cover of an old book,
Its contents torn out,
And stripped of its lettering and gilding)
Lies here food for worms ;
Yet the work itself shall not be lost,
For it will, as he believed, appear once more
In a new
And more beautiful edition,
Corrected and amended
by
the Author

Many of the earlier epitaphs were, however, written by the poetasters who earned a precarious living by writing love-sonnets and epitaphs and often also by acting as itinerant pedlars.

Puns on names and occupations were considered works of genius, as were also acrostics and anagrams. The quaint humour of these epitaphs was rarely intended, and arises chiefly from its incongruity. Relatives, too, seem to have found in gravestone inscriptions an opportunity for latent talent, and to have taken considerable pride in setting forth the virtues—or as is sometimes the case—the demerits of the deceased in verse.

Wordsworth did not write many epitaphs, but the following bathetic verses inscribed on a monument to Jemima Ann Deborah, second daughter of Sir Egerton Bridges, who died at the Ivy Cottage, Rydal, are from his pen :—

> These vales were saddened by no common gloom
> When good Jemima perished in her bloom.
> When, such the awful will of Heaven, she died
> By flames breathed on her from her own fireside.
> On earth we dimly see, and but in part
> We know, yet faith sustains the sorrowing heart :
> And she the pure, the patient and the weak,
> Might have fit epitaph could feelings speak :
> If words could tell and monuments record,
> How treasures lost are invariably deplored,
> No name for grief's fond eloquence adorned
> More than Jemima's would be praised and mourned
> The tender virtues of her blameless life,
> Bright in the daughter, brighter in the wife ;
> And in the cheerful mother brightest shone
> That light hath past away—the will of God be done.

Among the more recent examples of beautiful epitaphs the following epitaph on General Joubert, written by Rudyard Kipling, after our gallant enemy's death, is one of the finest tributes to a brave foe in the English language :—

With those that bred, with those that loosed the strife,
    He had no part whose hands were clear of gain ;
But, subtle, strong and stubborn, gave his life
    To a lost cause, and knew the gift was vain.

Later shall rise a people, sane and great,
    Forged in strong fires, by equal war made one,
Telling old battles over without hate—
    Noblest his name shall pass from sire to son.

He shall not meet the onsweep of our van
    In the doomed city when we close the score,
Yet o'er his grave—his grave that holds a man—
    Our deep-tongued guns shall answer his once more.

Perhaps the best pun—a touching and beautiful pun—
ever achieved in a self-epitaph is that on a grave in South
Africa. On the night before Spion Kop, Child, of South
African Horse, gave instructions that *when* (not *if*) he
fell on the morrow the words " It is well with the Child "
should be graven on his tombstone.

The beautiful epitaph written for himself by Robert
Louis Stevenson and now inscribed on the monument
over his grave at Samoa, is well known :—

    Under the wide and starry sky,
    Dig the grave and let me lie.
    Glad did I live and gladly die,
        And I laid me down with a will.

    This be the verse you grave for me :
    " Here he lies where he longed to be,
    Home is the sailor, home from sea,
        And the hunter home from the hill."

It is a singular fact that there is no monument to Sir
Christopher Wren, the builder of St. Paul's and of many
of the City Churches. Over the North door of the

Cathedral there is, however, a tablet with this inscription in Latin :—

Reader, if you seek his monument, look around.

A few days before John Keats died of decline at Rome, a gentleman who was sitting by his bedside, spoke of an inscription to his memory. Keats desired that there should be no mention of his name or country. "If there be anything," he said, "let it be :

"'Here lies the body of one whose name was
writ in water.'"

The difficulty of attempting any classification of a collection of epitaphs is enormous. As most of these are dated it was not thought necessary to place them in chronological order. I have, therefore, divided them into three sections, viz. Ancient Epitaphs, containing most of those until the end of the 17th Century; miscellaneous, including the more modern; and Quaint and Humorous, in which I have inserted many of the most curious of the ancient epitaphs.

In some of the older epitaphs, which were in Latin, I have given the accepted English translation, and where the ancient English spelling would have been confusing to the general reader, I have put it into more modern English.

ANCIENT EPITAPHS

ANCIENT EPITAPHS

THIS selection of verified ancient epitaphs I have preferred to put in a section of its own, though many of them would have been justified under the heading of Quaint and Humorous Epitaphs, on account of their unconscious and in most cases, unpremeditated humour. The frequency of plays upon names and occupations will be noted as well as the numerous acrostics and anagrams. Some of the epitaphs are by no means eulogistic and would, of course, not be tolerated in these times.

I have not attempted to reproduce the ancient spellings and old-time characters where these would be confusing to the general reader, for whom this book is intended rather than for the antiquarian. For the same reason I have reproduced many interesting Latin epitaphs in the English translation.

There has been little attempt at classification, but as most are dated they will afford some indication of the methods of expression at different periods down to the end of the seventeenth century.

Devonshire is peculiarly rich in quaint and homely epitaphs, especially in the village churchyards.

HALCOMBE-ROGUS, DEVON.

Nor goodness, nor desert, must hope to have
A privilege of life against the grave,
For those lie here entombed ; death did his best,
It changed but hours of evil for hours of rest :
Which this good man hath found.   His faith made way
To Heaven before : His works still day by day,
Now follow him : Such grace doth mercy give,
And who lives well to die, dies well to live.

15

A modest matron here doth lie
    A mirror of her kind
Her husband and her children's good,
    Her like is rare to find.
Godly, chaste and hospitable
    A housewife rare was she.

Ye poor she often would relieve
    Yet would not wasteful be
Her death a pattern was to die
    Her life was good likewise :
Her life and death assure her friends
    That she to joy shall rise.

1614.   Richard and Mary Bluett.

Exeter Cathedral.

As when a curious clock is out of frame
A workman takes in pieces small the same
And mending what amiss is to be found
The same rejoins and makes it true and sound.
So God this lady into two parts took
Too soon her soul her mortal corse forsook
But by His might at length her body found
Shall rise rejoined unto her soul new crowned
Till then they rest on earth and heaven sundered
At which conjoined all such as live we the wondered.

1614.   Dorothy Doddridge.

Stoke St. Nectan, Devon.

If long consuming sickness be a death,
I was long dead before I gave my breath :
But if in hopeful issue parents live
I'm not half dead, my best part doth survive.
There's no life lost, my progeny hath this
My soul a better life enjoys in bliss.

1601.   Nicholas Luttrell.

OTTERY ST. MARY, DEVON.

> Apollo moist this tomb with tears
> For such great loss in tender years
> Virtue's hope now is dead.
> And fro' earth to heaven is fled.
> Wit's perfection with poor spirit
> Doth an Angel's place inherit.
> Stay in that celestial sky
> Where thou shalt live and never die.
>
> 1620.   *Sarah Haydon.*

> Under this monument lies one
> Did good to many, hurt to none.
> Mended the rich, relieved the poor,
> Was kind to all—who can do more ?
>   That loved Hospitality,
>   Yet hated Prodigality.
>
> 1617.   *John Sherman.*

CLYST ST. GEORGE, DEVON.

> Bonifant a Virgin ; Osborne a loyal wife
> For thirty years ; A widow was forty and more.
> A hundred years almost she lead her life,
> Kind to the rich and good to the poor.
> Here lies her dust whose soul's to Heaven gone,
> Since she did live and die a saintlike one.
>
> 1614.   *Juliana Osborne.*

BERRYNARBOR, DEVON.

> Dedicated
> to the precious memory of
> Mary, the dear and only daughter of
> George Westcott pastor of this Church
> and of Frances his wife, who leaving
> this vale of misery for a mansion in
> felicity was here interred January 31, 1848.
> Aged 7

LANDKEY, DEVON.

Madam, to say you're dead were but to tell
A lie, or make the Poet Infidel.
You in your virtue live immortal that
Free from the dart of death, or stroke of fate,
You in your children live, your progeny,
And thro' a kind of Immortality,
Your body but doth sleep, your grave's a bed
Your stone a pillow, whereon to lie your head ;
Till Virtue, Children, body, soul, anon
Shall all meet in the Resurrection.

1645. *Elinor, Lady Vincent.*

MEMBURY, DEVON.

This tomb's sublimed to a shrine and doth contain
An holier Saint than could all legends fame,
Whose virtues supersede our spice and balm
Whose name perfumes the breath it sounds the same
As when a fly's involved in amber, 'twere
Less gain than pride such sepulchre,
So life's not worth such honours as to have
Fame write his epitaph, hearts afford his grave.

1645. *Sir Shilston Calmady.*

BECTON, DEVON.

His earthly part within this tomb doth rest,
Who kept a Court of Honour in his breast ;
Birth, Beauty, Wit, and Wisdom sat as Peers,
Till death mistook his virtues for his years ;
Or else Heaven envied Death so rich a treasure
Wherein too fine the Wave, too scant the measure.
His mournful wife her love to show in part,
This tomb built here, a better in her heart :
Sweet Babe, his hopeful heir, (heaven grant this boon)
Live but so well ; but oh ! die not so soon.

1638. *Denys Rolle. Aged* 24.

Abbot's Kerswell, Devon.

Here is a play on the name of the deceased.

Mason, how is't that thou so soon art gone
Home from thy work ? what, was the fault i'th'stone
Or did thy hammer fail, or dids't suspect
The Master's wages would thy work neglect !
Christ was thy *Corner Stone,* Christians the rest ;
Hammer the Word, good life they live all blest
And yet art gone, 'twas honour not thy crime
With stone hearts to work much in little time.
The Master savest, and took thee off from them
To the Wright stones of New Jerusalem.
Thy work and labour men esteem a base one
God counts it blest. Here lies a blest *Free Mason.*
                         1639. *Rev. William Mason.*

Totnes, Devon.

Here lieth Grace a flower gay,
Far passing all the flowers of May,
Even at the Spring-time of the year
Was pluckt, and feicht as fit to be
In hands of highest majesty.
Then let us praise God for this
That she is crowned with endless bliss.
                    1636. *Grace Grylls.*

Calverleigh, Devon.

Here in one bed of earth asleep do lie
Three generations, for they did not die,
Nor lose a being, but exchanged, and must
At the trump's sound awaken out of this dust.
Here's but their corps, in heaven their souls do dwell,
Live here, so to live there with them, Farewell.
1638. *George Southcote, Thomas and Mary Southcote and*
                    Mary Colman their daughter.

St. Saviour's, Dartmouth.

> Behold thyself by me
> I was as thou art now
> And thou in time shalt be
> When dust as I am now.
> So doth this figure paint to thee
> The form and state of each degree.
>
> 1637.   *Gilbert Staplehill, ex-Mayor.*

Ilfracombe.

This is a somewhat elaborate epitaph beginning with a Greek motto, followed by anagrams on the names of husband and wife. Next is a rather far-fetched acrostic on both Christian and surnames, and then these verses.

> Charles sounds of Fortitude yet courteous he ;
> Unto all sorts seemed rather still to be
> Her name and disposition joined in one :
> Though name behind yet Grace with her is gone.
> These two so lived and loved together,
> That Death itself could not them sever,
> One bed, one board, gave them content :
> And now one grave with free consent
> Whose bodies here interred were,
> Their souls (we hope), Celestial are
> Who still were friends unto the best
> And that with such they now do rest.
>
> 1637.   *Charles and Grace Cutliffe.*

Shayford, Devon.

> Reader, woulds't know who here is laid ?
> Behold a Matron, yet a maid :
> A modest look, a pious heart,
> A Mary for the better part :
> But dry thine eyes, why wilt thou weep ?
> Such damsels do not die but sleep.
>
> 1641.   *Mary Whiddon.*

ASHBURTON, DEVON.

> Fear not to die,
> Learn this of me,
> No fear in death
> If good thou be.
>
> 1637.   *Thomas Harris.*

ARLINGTON, DEVON.

> Here lies Will Burgoin, a Squire by descent
> Whose death in this world many people lament :
> The rich for his love,
> The poor for his alms
> The wife for his knowledge
> The sick for his balms.
> Grace he did love and vice control
> Earth hath his body and Heaven his soul
> The twelfth day of August in the morn died he
> One six and two three.
>
> 1623.   *William Burgoin.*

WEARE GIFFARD, DEVON.

On a monument erected in honour of the Fortescue Family. At the top is an eye surrounded by clouds with issuing rays; beneath kneeling figures, and medallions containing busts of several generations of children.

> Stay, Reader, stay, this structure seems t'invite
> Thy wandering eyes, on it to fix thy sight.
> In this Pile's summit thou mayest descry
> Heaven's all beholding and all guiding eye
> That sheds his benedictions gracious beams
> Of Love and Goodness on these fruitful streams
> Of numerous issue, sprung from nuptial ties
> With various ancient worthy families.
> Here is in brief presented to thy view
> The long liv'd race of honoured *Fortescue.*
> Combined in holiest rites, on Time's fair scroll

With *Chichester*, then *Speccott*, last with *Rolle*.
And long and wide may sacred Grace and Fame
Produce and propagate this generous name
That it may brook what Honour gave in field
Le fort Escue, the strong and lasting Shield.
A shield not only their own right to fence,
But also to repel wrong's violence
Which, that it may accordingly be done
Pray, Reader, pray God be their Shield and Sun.

1625 *circa.*

ASHBURTON, DEVON.

Within this space two brothers here confined,
Though by death parted, yet by death close joined ;
The eldest of the two ; placed in his tomb,
Greeted the younger with a welcome home.
They lived, they loved, and now rest in tomb
Together sleeping in their mother's womb.

1649.   *Thomas and George Cruse.*

HEANTON-PUNCHARDON, DEVON.

Thy ashes here : but in my mind
Thy love and worth I have enshrin'd
Sleep dust then till my soul in state
Descend to fetch hence its old mate
When cloth'd with glory both shall shine
For ever Christ's which once were mine.

1651.   *Sarah Colenore.*

BISHOP'S TAWTON, DEVON.

A Rose's springing branch no sooner bloomed
By Death's impartial dart lies here entombed
Tho' wither'd be the bud, the stock relies
On Christ both sure by faith and hope to rise.

1652.   *Rose Dart (an infant).*

BARNSTAPLE.

> Reader, if thou wouldst know this gem that lies
> Cased in this marble, first ask the poors eyes
> Who that they may preserve their dear loss safe
> Write in their lasting tears his epitaph.
> Then read the School by him endowed t'advance
> Arts 'bove monster teeming ignorance.
> If next you'd learn the prudence of the gown
> And whom he held the scales, ask the whole town—
> But lastly, view this place, which though it is
> God's house by right, his zeal yet made it his.
> Here would he live—here he full oft hath been
> To speak to God and hear God speak to him.
> So that to write his epitaph must be
> To picture Justice, Arts, Faith, Charity
> Let marble quarries then elsewhere be spent
> Not stones but deeds built up this monument.
> Reader, this tomb speaks not unto thy eyes
> But to thy hands—go thou and do likewise.

> 1649.   *Richard Ferris, twice Mayor of Barum.*

CALVERLEIGH, DEVON.

> Under this tombstone know there lies
> A dainty youth of richest price,
> Soon cropt by death while under age
> Through fever's violence and rage
> Earth keeps his body in restraint
> But Heaven owns him for a saint.

> 1654.   *George Southcott.   Aged* 15.

BRANSCOMBE, DEVON.

> The wine that in these earthen vessels lay
> The hand of Death has lately drawn away :
> And as a present sent it up on high
> Whilst here the Vessels with the lees doth lie.

> 1658.   *On a father and son named Vessels.*

c

HACCOMBE, DEVON.

> Here lieth the bodies of Thomas Carew Esquire
> and Anne his wife who deceased the 6th and
> 8th day of December anno domini 1656.

> Two bodies lie beneath this stone
> Whom love and marriage long made one
> One soul conjoined them by a force
> Above the power of death's divorce
> One flame of love their lives did burn
> Even to ashes in their urn
> They die but not depart who meet
> In wedding and in winding sheet
> Whom God hath knit so firm in one
> Admit no separation
> Therefore unto one marble trust
> We leave their now united dust
> As roots on earth embrace to rise
> Most lovely flowers in Paradise.

1656.

HEANTON-PUNCHARDON, DEVON.

> Here sleeps a noble pair who were in life
> He best of husbands, she of wives the wife.

1660.   *John and Susanna Bassett.*

BARNSTAPLE.

> 'Tis not her plenteous issue, nor this pile
> Her husband's love erected can beguile
> Times 'stroying hand : for such memorials must
> Themselves lie down, wrapt in oblivion's dust.
> No, she preferred her name, a way more sure
> By Faith, Love, Patience, a meek life and pure
> These, these are spices shall embalm her name
> And make it fragrant when the world's aflame.

1656.   *Mrs. Amy Tooker.*

ALWINGTON, DEVON.

All here portrayed shows one joined Coffin ! sent
Through heavens canopy and to earth here lent
Perfumed with virtues and bedewed with grace
T'adorn them with a progeny for a space
One man took life from dead Elisha's bones
Eight martial sons lived from this Coffin's loins
With daughters seven yet from this vine did sprout
Like olive plants their table round about
Thrice happy fruitful Coffin, may thy buds spring
And to eternity hallelujahs sing.

1651.   *Richard Coffin and Elizabeth his wife.*

KENTON, DEVON.

Surpassing the philosopher's, this stone
Shall turn to pearls the tears are dropt thereon,
Since to praise worth praiseworthy doth appear
This shrine makes saints of them which offer here
Their spice and balm for too perfume his name
Which rather more perfumed are by the same.

1653.   *Sir Nicholas Martyn.*

MONKLEIGH, DEVON.

Since epitaphs have given speech to stones,
Their Rhetoric extorted sighs tears groans :
Some teach Divinity ; but this commends :
Dries tears, stops sighs, and strangleth groans of friends
Oxford's Academic so prized his parts :
That it did crown him Laureate of Arts :
In country he read men, in Court the laws,
Lived both with sweet contentment and applause :
Expir'd by degrees : yet our comfort's this
That death his convoy was from pain to bliss :
Since Temperance, Prudence, Candour, Pity
Transports from Grace unto Felicity.

1651.   *William Gaze.*

Swimbridge, Devon.

> Lo with a *Warrant* sealed by God's Decree
> Death his grim *Sergeant* hath *arrested* me,
> No *Bail* was to be given, no *Law* could save
> My body from the prison of the grave.
> Yet by the Gospel my poor soul had got
> A *Superfedeus*, and Death seized it not.
> And for my downcast body here it lies,
> A prisoner of Hope it shall arise.
> Faith doth assure me, God of His great love
> In Christ shall send a *Writ* for my *Remove*,
> And set my body, as my soul is, free
> With Christ to dwell.   Come glorious Liberty.

1658.   John Raster, Attorney.

East Allington, Devon.

> Eliza's soul, a graft divine
> With clay was fastened unto Wood !
>   The tree did suddenly decline
>   The fruit was blasted in the bud.
> The clay which Death broke off lies here, the wife
> Is now engrafted on the Tree of Life.
> Reader, expect not long to hold thy breath
> For heart of oak thou seest cut off by death.

1662.   Elizabeth Wood.

Ilfracombe.

> Never was Innocence and Prudence
> So lovely, that had you known her
> Conversation, you would have said
> She was the daughter of Eve before
> She eated of the Apple.

> She hath left her name
> Catherine Parminter
> A.D. 1660.

COLYTON, DEVON.

>Such pillars laid aside
>How can the church abide
>He left his pulpit he
>In Patmas God to see
>This shining light can have
>No place to preach but's grave.

>> 1667.   *Rev. John Williams.*

CHITTLEHAMPTON, DEVON.

>The Graces formerly were counted three,
>Now to the count a fourth may added be,
>The Virgin that of graces had such store
>As she made good her name of Grace and more.
>Her loving parents were to her so dear
>They going hence she'd stay no longer here.
>But after hies (blest soul) to heaven above,
>To be with them in the family of love,
>And by their bodies here must lie to rest
>That with them she may rise together blest.

>> 1667.   *Mrs. Grace Giffard.*

ASHBURTON, DEVON.

>His pious soul wrapped in distempered earth
>Was now prepared for a second birth ;
>He straight ascending the celestial spheres,
>Cast off her mantle, and hath left it here.

>> 1643.   *Robert Gaunter, Gent.*

HEAVITREE, DEVON.

>The loving turtle having missed her mate
>Begged she might enter ere they shut the gate
>Their dust here lies whose souls to Heaven are gone
>And wait till Angels roll away the stone.

>> 1671.   *Thomas and Rose Gorges.*

Dean Prior, Devon.

No trust to metals nor to marbles when
These have their fate and wear away as men !
Times, titles, trophies, may be lost and spent :
But virtue rears th' eternal monument.
What more than these can tombs or tombstones pay ?
But here's the sunset of a tedious day ;
These two asleep are, I'll but be undressed
And so to bed : pray with us all good rest.

1637.   *Sir Edward and Lady Giles.*

Seaton, Devon.

John Starre
Starr on high !
Where should a starr be
But on high ?
Tho' underneath
He now doth lie
Sleeping in Dust
Yet shall he rise
More glorious than
The Starres in skies.

1633. *John Starre.*

Bittadon, Devon.

A generous mind, a stout courageous heart,
A man well stored with policy, wit and art ;
In feats of war and law he did abound
As scarce beyond him any could be found.
What could be learnt both here and 'yond the main
He in's vast memory strongly did retain.
A well experienced man in all affairs
He such a name 'mongst us surviving bears.
His body is here below, his soul is fled
Whither the winged cherubims are fed.

1691.   *Edward Poyntz.*

WIDDECOMBE-IN-THE-MOOR, DEVON.
To the Memorie of
Mary the third wife of John Elford of Shistor, Esq.
was here interred Febr. ye 16, 1642, having issue
at a birth Mary and Sarah.

As Mary's choice made John rejoice
So was her loss his heavy cross most know
Yet lost she is not save but found above
Death gave her life t'embrace a dearer love
(Anagr.)   Mary Elford—Fear my Lord—
Then Fear my Lord whilst yet you mayest on mold
That so those arms that me may thee enfold
Near twelve months day her marriage here did pass
Her heavenly nuptial consummated was
She fertile proved in sould and body both
In life good works and death the twins brought forth
And like a fruitful tree with bearing died
Yet Phœnix like for one these two survived
Which shortly posted their dear mother after
Least this contagion their poor souls might slaughter
Then cease your sad laments I am but gone
To reap above what I below have sown.

KINGS TEIGNTON, DEVON.
Damn'd tyrant, can't profaner blood suffice ?
Must Priests that offer be the sacrifice ?
Go, tell the genii that in Hades lie,
Thy triumps o'er this sacred Calvary,
Till some just Nemesis avenge our Cause
And force this kill-priest to reverse good laws.
1670.   *Richard Adlam.*

MORCHARD BISHOP, DEVON.
Grace, sweetness, beauty,—yet not touched with pride
She lived beloved, and much lamented died.
1690.   *Hannah Wheeler.*

DARTMOUTH, DEVON.

> Men that are virtuous serve the Lord :
> And the devil's by his friends adored :
> And as they merit get a place
> Amidst the blest of hellish race.
> Pray then, ye learned clergy, show
> Where can this brute, Tom Goldsmith, go ?
> Whose live was one continued evil,
> Striving to cheat God, man and devil.

> 1714.   *Thomas Goldsmith, a noted pirate.*

BRAUNTON, DEVON.

> Here lieth interred Mrs. Deborah Keene
> late owner of the Manor of Braunton-Arundell in
> this parish.   She was baptised Feb. 24, 1624,
> lived unmarried, and was buried Dec. 31, 1694.

> Virginity was had in estimation
> And wont to be observed with veneration :
> *Above* 'tis still so, single life is fed,
> None may marry nor are married,
> But live angelic lives : and Virgins crowned
> All with their Coronets the Lamb surround.
> This maiden Landlay hath one obtained,
> Who tho' much sought in marrying still refrained,
> And now the inheritance undefiled has gained.

> 1694.   *Deborah Keene.*

MEMBURY, DEVON.

> Stop passenger, and view this mournful shrine,
> That holds the relics of a form divine :
> Oh ! she was all perfection, heavenly fair !
> And chaste and innocent as mortals are.
> Her wit and humour and her youth conspired
> To warm the soul, and all who saw admired !—
> But ah ! how soon was all the heaven of charms

Rifled by death, and withered in his arms ;
Too soon for us, but not for her too soon !
For now upon the wings of angels flown
Their native skies, she's by her God caressed
And keeps eternal Sabbath with the blessed.
Learn hence, betimes, (good reader) to be wise
This trifling world and all its joys despise.
With each bright virtue let thy bosom swell,
And live like her, that you may do so well.

1723. *Frances Fry.*

TIVERTON, DEVON.

On helpless babes I did attend
Whilst I on earth my life did spend :
To help the helpless in their need
I ready was with care and speed.
Many from pain my hands did free
But none from death could rescue me
My course is run and hour is passed
And you is coming also fast.

John Bradley was the first child she received
Into this world in 1698, and since, above 5,000.

1733. *Mrs. Ann Clarke.*

WEST ALLINGTON, DEVON.

This youth when in his sickness lay,
Did for the minister send that he
Would come and with him pray but
he would not attend but when this
young man buried was the minister
did him admit he should be carried
into Church that he might money get
By this you see what man will do
to get money if he can who did refuse
to come and pray by the foresaid young man.

1746. *Daniel Jeffrey.*

ILFRACOMBE, DEVON.

> Joan Ley here she lays all mould in grave
> I trust in God her soul to save
> And with her Saviour Christ to dwell
> And there I hope to live as well.

> This composed by her grateful husband
> Nicholas Ley.

1759. *Joan Ley.*

HADLEIGH, SUFFOLK.

> To free me from domestic strife
> Death called at my house, but he spake with my wife
> Susan, wife of David Pattison lies here,
> Stop Reader, and if not in a hurry, shed a tear.

1706.   *Susan Pattison.*

CROYLAND, LINCS.

> Beneath this place in 6 foot in length against the
> Clark's Pen lieth the body of
> Mr. Abm. Baby
> Also the body of Mary his wid.
> She died the 21st May 1705
> Also 2 children of the said Abm. and Mary, which
> died in their infantry.

> Man's life is like unto a winter's day,
> Some break their fast, and so depart away.
> Other's stay dinner—then depart full fed,
> The longest age but sups and goes to bed.
> O reader, then behold and see
> As we are now so must ye be.

1706.

STOKE ST. NECTAN, DEVON.

> Stay awhile you passers by
> And see how I in dust do lie
> Tho' I lie here in confusing mould
> I shall rise up like shining gold.

> 1720. *Henry Wilcock.*

This is a popular idea in epitaphs, and variations are to be found in several churchyards.

OAKHAM, RUTLAND.

> Farewell poor world, I must be gone,
> Thou art no home, no rest for me,
> I'll take my staff and travel on
> Till I a better world may see
> Put on, my soul, put on with speed
> Tho' the way be long, the end is near :
> Once more, poor world, farewell indeed.

> (The last line is illegible.)

> 1707. *James Marshall.*

NORTH STONEHAM, HANTS.

> I hope, I think, I understand
> Here lies the body of an honest man.
> I trust in Christ and hope that he
> The joys of Heaven now do see.

> 1708. *John Vine.*

FINEDON, NORTHANTS.

> Here lieth Richard Dent
> in his last tenement.

> 1709.

TETBURY, GLOS.

> Her body earthly was, and to the Earth
> Descended is, from whence it took its birth.
> Her soul from a more high Original
> Mounted aloft, became Angelical
> Clog not her wings, then, with your dewy tears
> On which she's raised above the starry spheres
> Cease, Husband, Children, cease, give God the praise
> Which now she warbles in immortal lays.
>
> > 1710.   *Mary Cripps.*

CANTLEY, NORFOLK.

> In wise frugality luxuriant,
> In Justice and good Acts extravagant,
> To all the world an universal friend,
> No foe to any but the savage kind
> How many fair estates have been graced
> By the same generous means : yet has increased
> His duty thus performed to Heaven and Earth
> Each leisure hour fresh toilsome sports gave birth,
> Had Nimrod seen, he would the game decline
> To *Gilbert* mighty hunter's name resign
> Tho' hundreds to the grounds he oft has chased,
> That subtle fox Death earthed him here at last,
> And left a fragrant scent so sweet behind
> That ought to be pursued by all mankind.
>
> > 1714.   *Robert Gilbert.*

STROUD, GLOS.

> > When Christ commands away
> > 'Tis sin to wish to stay
> > 'Tho soon thy glass be run
> > For Heaven thou'rt not too young
> > For all are like thee there
> > Go then, and be Heaven's heir.
> >
> > > *Freame Clutterbuck, an infant.*

Ripon, Yorks.

Here lieth the body of Margaret Lupton, late wife of Mr. Sampson Lupton of Braisty Woods in Netherdale, who departed this life the 2nd of November Anno Domini 1718 in the 74th year of her age, and lived to be mother and grandmother to above 150 children, and at the baptizing of the first grandchild, the child had ten grandfathers and grandmothers then present.

Welton, Yorks.

Here lieth the old
Jeremy who hath
eight times married
been but now in his
old age he lies
in his cage under
the grass so green
Which Jeremiah Simp
Son departed this
Life in the 84 years
of his age in the
year of our Lord
1719

Jeremiah Simpson.

Ombersley, Worc.

Sharp was her wit, mild was her nature :
A tender wife and a good humoured creature.

1724. *Elizabeth Cupper.*

West Down, Devon.

Reader, pass on, nor waste your precious time
On bad biography and murdered rhyme :
What I was before's well known to my neighbours
What I am now is no concern of yours.

1797. *William Ash.*

Pilton, Devon.

'Tis done, the last great debt of nature paid,
Hayne amongst the numerous dead is laid :
O'er hills and dales, thro' woods, o'er mountains, rocks,
With keenest ardour he pursued the Fox !
Heedless of dangers, stranger to dismay,
Dauntless thro' obstacles he held his way !
But now, alas ! no more his bosom beats
High in the chase, forgotten are his heats ;
His ardor boots him not, for here are bounds
Ne'er overleap'd by huntsman or by hounds ;
Here was his course arrested : then draw near
Sons of the Chase, and drop the pitying tear :
Now o'er his tomb as you impassioned bend,
And pensive think of your departed friend,
Repeat the tale conveyed in simple strain,
And sighing say—here lies poor honest Hayne.

1797.   *John Hayne.*

St. Petrock's, Dartmouth.

'Twas not a winded nor a withered face
Nor long gray hairs, nor dimness in the eyes,
Nor feeble limbs, nor uncouth trembling pace,
Presaged his death that here entombed lies :
His time was come, his Maker was not bound
To let him live till all these marks were found.
His time was come, that time he did embrace
With sense and feeling, with a joyful heart,
As his first passage to a better place,
Where all his cares are ended and his smart
This Roope was blessed that trusted in God alone :
He lives two lives where others live but one.

1609.   *John Roope.*

Wiltshire also furnishes a large number of quaint ancient epitaphs of which the following selection is representative.

AVEBURY, WILTS.

Come near my friends, behold and see
Such as I am such shall you be :
As is my state within this tomb
So must yours be before the doom.
For all men must by God's decree
Once taste of death as ye see me.
Wherefore in time remember Death
Before you lose your vital breath
John Truslove here interred is,
And lieth in this grave :
Which unto me large benefits
Most bountifully gave.
The race he lived here on earth
Was three score years and seven
Deceased in April 93 and then
        Was prest to Heaven.
He having then no issue left
        His loving wholly gave
To Richard Truslove of his name
        For so he would it have.
Who in remembrance of the giver
This stone has caused to be
Within this Church of Averbarie
Erected as you see.

The body of John Truslove here doth rest
Who dying did his soul to heaven bequest :
His faith in Christ most steadfastly was it,
In saved hope to satisfy his debt.
A lively theme to take example by
Contemming death in hope a Saint to die.

                    1593. *John Truslove.*

COLLINGBOURNE DUCIS, WILTS.

> Speechless tho' yet he were, say all we can
> That saw, he promise did a hopeful man
> Such frame of body, such a holy soul
> Argu'd him written in the long-liv'd roll
> But now we see, by such an infant's loss
> All are but infant hopes, which death may cross.

1631.   *Edward St. Maur, infant son of the Earl of Hereford.*

POTTERNE, WILTS.

> Here lies Mary, the wife of John Ford,
> We hope her soul is gone to the Lord ;
> But if for Hell she has chang'd this life
> She had better be there than be John Ford's wife.

1790.   *Mary Ford.*

BISHOP'S CANNINGS, WILTS.

> Farewell, vain world, I know enough of thee
> And now am careless what thou say'st of me
> Thy smiles I envy not nor thy frowns fear
> My cares are past, my head lies quiet here.
> What faults you've seen in me, take care to shun
> And look at home.   Enough there's to be done.

1792.   *Isaac Smith.*

BROUGHTON-GIFFORD, WILTS.

Here is another play on the name of the deceased.

> The life of man is a true lottery,
> Where venturous death draws forth lots short and long :
> Yet free from fraud and partial flattery
> He shuffled shields of several size among,
> Drew *Longe* ; and so drew longer his short days
> Th' Ancient of days beyond all time to praise.

1620.   *Robert Longe.*

DINTON, WILTS.

And here is another on a man named Earth.

From Earth we came, to earth we must return
Witness this Earth that lies within this Urn.
Begot by Earth : born also of Earth's womb,
74 years lived Earth, now earth's his tomb
In earth Earth's body lies under this stone
But from this earth to Heaven Earth's soul is gone.

1634.   *Roger Earth.*

BROMHAM, WILTS.

And here is still another. It seems to have been a favourite form of epitaph in Wilts.

Here lies an heir who to an Heir was joined,
And dieing left a little Heir behind.
Hard hearted Death herein was somewhat mild,
He took the mother but he spared the child.
Yet th' one's more happy far than is the other,
The child's an Heir on earth, in Heaven the mother,
Where with triumphant Saints and Angels bright
She now enjoys the blessed Saviour's sight.

1637.   *Elizabeth Eyre.*

PEWSEY, WILTS.

Stay awhile and spend a tear
Upon the dust that slumbers here
And while thou read'st the fate of me
Think on the glass that runs for thee.
I grieve to think I cannot grieve no more
To think my dearest friend is gone before
But since it pleased God to part us here
In Heaven I hope to meet my dearest Dear.

1745.   *Samuel and Mary Austen.*

D

HOLT, WILTS.

> This stony register is for her bones
> Her fame is more perpetual than the stones :
> And still her goodness, tho' herself be gone,
> Shall live when earth thy monuments are gone.
> Who reading this can choose but drop a tear
> For such a loving wife and mother dear.

1646.   *Annie Bailey.*

POTTERNE, WILTS.   1715.

This epitaph, with slight variations, is found all over the country.

> Remember man as you
> Pass by as you are now
> So once was I as I am
> Now so must you be
> Make peace with Christ
> And follow me
> Fear God and keep his Command
> Ment this is the whole duty of
> Man.

DINTONE, WILTS.

The parents of this boy seem to have a grievance tho' they do not state what it is.

> Here lies dear John, his parent's love and joy,
> That most pretty and ingenious boy,
> His matchless soul is not yet forgotten
> Though here the lovely boddy dead and rotten
> Ages to come may wonder at his fame,
> And here his death by shameful malice came.
> How spiteful some did use him and how rude
> Grief will not let me write : but now conclude
> To God for ever all praise be given
> Since we hope he is with him in Heaven.

1716.   *John Aske.*

CRUDWELL, WILTS.

This is one of the briefest epitaphs extant.

> Received of Philip Harding
> his borrowed earth.
> July 4th, 1673.

LEGH DELAMERE, WILTS.

> Death in a good old age
> Ended our weary pilgrim stage
> It was to we a end of pain
> In hopes to enter Life again.

> 1764. *John and Alice Browning.*

HOLT, WILTS.

> Tho here Engrave our Son so dear is laid
> If God had pleased for him with us to stayed
> Until our eyes with his had closed been
> Then had not us these days of sorrow seen.

> 1771. *John Biffey.*

PEWSEY, WILTS.

> Death in a good old age
> Ended my weary pilgrimage
> The time was come to rise, and then
> I hope to be with Christ, Amen.

> 1776. *Richard Hooper.*

NETTLECOMBE, SOMERSET.

> Much of my welfare and content below
> I to my mother's love and virtues owe :
> Wherefore this humble grave so near her bones
> I more esteem than elsewhere marble stones.

> 1648. *John Musgrave.*

FORRABURY, CORNWALL.

Under this Tomb a female Gourd doth lie
Was only born to have that name and die
She from the womb unto the grave was sent
In a few days : yet this as Punishment
But happiness that she a race hath run
To Ease : which some have scarce begun
And be at once a rising and a setting sun
Set, did I say, No, she doth shine more clear
But in another orb, another sphere :
Oh happy thou, thrice happy thou
Who n'eer didst know
What 'twas to make or break thy vow
Nor thou unto no sin didst ever fall
But that we mortals term original
Which though it wound the soul the first was pure
Our Saviour's blood will prove His sovereign cure
Sweet innocence thou in no seas wast tost
Nor in a wilderness an age was lost
Till to the promised Canaan thou didst come
All pious men's the patriarchs and thy home
O had I but my wish then I should be
Soon or at last sweet Saint to be with thee.

1671.   *Katherine Gourd.*

ALL SAINTS', BRISTOL.

The subject of this epitaph was " twice Master of the Company of Bakers," hence the allusions.

Like to a Baker's oven is the grave
Wherein the bodies of the faithful have
A Setting in : and where they do remain
In hopes to Rise, and to be drawn again :
Blessed are they who in the Lord are dead
Though Set like Dough, they shall be drawn like Bread.

1643.   *Thomas Turar.*

St. Enodes, Cornwall.

> Remember man within my youthful days
> To serve the Lord ere death thy body sieze
> then live to die to gain so high a prize
> that thy poor soul may live in Paradise
>
> Here is the love of wife shown
> That where we lie by this it may be known
> My wife and I did in love so well agree
> Yet must I part for God would have it so to be
> From my wife Ann Mahly.

> 1687. *John and Ann Mahly.*

Marsfield, Somerset.

* This epitaph, *circa* 1620, bears no Christian name or date.

> Life is the day of Grace, and Death the Night :
> Live well, who knows when he shall lose the light,
> So did the tenant of this tomb, for he
> Made haste to purchase immortality
> Death, finding him, receiving Customs, Lookes,
> Times, Records, summed his days, and crossed the Books.
> And now the Customer's from Customs free,
> He paid to Nature what her Duties be.
> Scarce had he ran out half his race of life,
> When Heaven and Earth to have him were at strife.
> Whose active soul wove out his flesh so nigh,
> 'Twas time she should the tired corpse lay by.
> To bad men death is sad : when good men die,
> It is then birth to joy's eternity.
> Judge then what he did lose who lost but breath
> Lived to die well, and died a *Meredeth.*

* A similar inscription is on an organist of St. Mary Winton College, Oxford.

LILLINGTON, DORSET.

Reader you have within this grave
A *Cole* raked up in dust :
His courteous fate saw it was late
And that to bed he must :
So all was swept up to be kept
Alive until the day
The trump should blow it up and show
   The *Cole* but sleeping lay.

Then do not doubt, the *Cole's* not out,
   Though it in ashes lies :
That little spark now in the dark
   Will like a Phœnix rise.

            1669.   *Thomas Cole.*

TITCHFIELD, HANTS.

The husband speaking truly of his wife
Read his loss in her death, her praise in her life.

Here Lucy Quinsy Bromfield buried lies
With neighbours weeping, hearts, sighs, eyes
Children eleven, ten living, me she brought
More kind, true, chaste, was none, in deed, word, thought,
House, children, estate, by her was ruled, bred, thrives
One of the best of maids, of women, wives,
Now gone to God, her heart sent long before ;
In fasting, prayer, faith, hope, and almsdeeds store
If any fault, she loved me too much
Ah ! pardon that, for there are too few such !
Then Reader, if thou not hard hearted be
Praise God for her, but sigh and pray for me.
   Here by her dead, I dead desire to be
   Till, raised to life, we meet no more to die.

            1618.   *Lucy Bromfield.*

BLIDWORTH, HANTS.

Here rests T. Leake whose virtues were so known
In all these parts, that this engraved stone
Needs nought relate but his untimely end
Which was in single fight : whilst youth did lend
His aid to valour, he with ease o'erpast
Many slight dangers greater than this last
But wilful fate in these things governs all
He told out threescore years before his fall :
Much of which time he wasted in this wood
Much of his wealth, and last of all his blood.

1608. *Thomas Leake.*

LOAD, SOMERSET.

Of John Hellierd, gentleman, who died this day
We that are living have just cause to say
That never man died more Christian like death
Which to us appeared even by his last breath.
As therefore his body doth hereunder rest
So doubtless his soul in heaven is blest.
For we find in the Scripture by sacred record
They blessed are they who die in the Lord.
God grant us all then His mercy and grace
So to end this life that in heaven we may have place
There to remain for ever and ever
With Abram and Isaac and this my dear father.

1623. *John Hellierd.*

ST. WERBURGH, BRISTOL.

Elizabeth White married Humphrey Brown, which gave
the writer of this epitaph his opportunity.

Here lies a *Brown*, a *White*, the colours one,
Pale drawn by death, here shaded by a stone :
One house did hold them both whilst life did last,
One grave doe hold them both now life is past.

1630. *Humphrey and Elizabeth Brown.*

DULOE, CORNWALL.

Anagrams are often found as the basis of epitaphs. Here
is an instance—rather far-fetched.

> Marya Arundell—Man a dry Laurel
> Man to the marigold compared may be,
> Then may be likened to the laurel tree
> Both feed the eye—both please the optic sense ;
> Both soon decay—both suddenly fleet hence :
> What then infer you from her name but this
> Man fades away—Man a dry Laurell is.

1629.

BERKELEY, GLOS.

> Here lieth Thomas Pierce whom no man taught
> Yet he on Iron, Brass, and Silver Wrought.
> He Jacks, and Clocks, and watches (with art) made
> And mended too when other's work did fade.
> Of Berkeley five times Mayor this artist was,
> And yet this Mayor, this Artist, was but grass.
> When his own watch was down the last day
> He that made watches had not made a Key
> To wind it up, but useless it must lie
> Until he rise again no more to die.

1635. Thomas Pierce. Aged 77.

ST. KATHERINE'S, GLOUCESTER.

On a much married man.

> Here lies old Mr. Richard Tully
> Who lived an C and 3 years fully,
> And threescore years before the Mayor
> The sword of this City he did bear.
> Nine of his wives do by him lie
> So shall the tenth when she doth die.

1725. Richard Tully.

SLIMBRIDGE, GLOS.

Here lies a Father with his offspring dear,
Joy of his heart and solace of his care :
She fresh in years and tender in her frame
Withered and fell by fever's wasteful flame.
The parent anxious to allay the fire,
Unguarded, stricken, did near her expire.
O gloomy state of man ! when void of fence
Not virtue stand, nor yet can Innocence !
But since the good awaits a better lot :
A child of God's can never be forgot.

Dr. Robert Awood and Elizabeth his daughter aged 7.

EPWORTH, LINC.

The epitaph of the Rev. Samuel Wesley, father of John
and Charles Wesley.   He died in 1735.

Here
Lieth all that was Mortal
of Samuel Wesley, A.M. he was
Rector of Epworth 39 years
and departed this life 25 of
April 1735 aged 72.

As he lived so he died in the
true Catholic Faith of the
Holy Trinity in Unity and
that Jesus Christ is God
Incarnate and the only Saviour
of Mankind Acts 4—12.

Blessed are the dead which
die in the Lord yea saith the
Spirit that they may rest
from their labours and their
works do follow them.

Rev. 14—13.

WOLVERHAMPTON.

Charles Claudius Philips, whose absolute contempt of riches and inimitable performances on the violin made him the admiration of all that knew him. He was born in Wales, made the tour of Europe, and after the experience of both kinds of fortune, died in the year 1723.

> Exalted soul, thy various sounds could please
> The lovesick virgin, and the gouty ease,
> And jarring crowds, like old Amphion, move
> To beauteous order and harmonious love.
> Now rest in peace, till Angels bid thee rise,
> And join thy Saviour's concert in the skies.

ASHTON, GLOS.

> Vain King of Terrors, boast no more
> Thine ancient wide extended power,
> Each Saint in life, with Christ his head
> Shall reign, when thou thyself art dead.
>
> *Edward Strange.*

OCKHAM, SURREY.

Here is a punning epitaph on a carpenter.

> Who many a sturdy oak had laid along,
> Fell'd by Death's surer hatchet, here lies Spong.
> Posts oft he made yet ne'er a place could get,
> And liv'd by railing, tho' he was no wit.
> Old saws he had, altho' no antiquarian,
> And styles corrected, yet no grammarian.
> Long liv'd he Ockham's prime architect :
> And lasting as his fame a tomb t'erect
> In vain we seek an artist such as he
> Whose pales and gates are for eternity.
>
> 1736. *John Spong, Carpenter.*

AYLESBURY, BUCKS.

And here is one on a blacksmith. This with slight variations is found in many churchyards.

> My sledge and hammer lie declined
> My bellows too have lost their wind.
> My fire's extinct, my forge decayed,
> And in the dust my vice is laid.
> My coal is spent, my iron's gone,
> My nails are drove, my work is done.
>
> 1745.   *Richard Austin.*

OCKHAM, SURREY.

> The Lord saw good, I was lopping off wood,
> And down fell from the tree :
> I met with a check, and I broke my neck
> And so death lopped off me.

RIPON, YORKS.

> Here Henry Raper
> lies in dust :
> His stature small
> His mind was just.
>
> 1728.

EASINGWOLD, YORKS.

This is a somewhat qualified eulogy.

Anne Harrison well known by the name of Nanna Ran Dan, who was chaste but no prude ; and tho' free yet no harlot. By principle virtuous, by education a Protestant ; her freedom made her liable to censure, while her extensive charities made her esteemed. Her tongue she was unable to control, but the rest of her members she kept in subjection. After a life of 80 years thus spent, she died 1745.

ST. GILES', SHREWSBURY.

> Here Charles Rathbone he doth lie
> And by a misfortune he did die
> On the 17th of July

> **1751.**

HASTINGS, SUSSEX.

> Good people as you pass by
> I pray you on me cast an eye
> For as you am so once was I
> And as I am so must you be
> Therefore prepare to follow **me.**

> 1751. *Joseph Dain.*

MELROSE, N.B.

> The earth goeth on the earth
> Glittering like gold
> The earth goeth to the earth
> Sooner than it would
> The earth builds on the earth
> Castles and Towers
> The earth says to the earth
>   All shall be ours.

> 1751. *James Ramsay.*

LESLIE, FIFE.

> Here lies in the dust Charles Brown
> Sometime a wright in London town
> Who coming home parents to see
> And of his years being twenty-three
> Of a decay with a bad host *
> He died upon the Yorkshire coast.
>   The 18th of May, 1752
> We hope his soul in Heaven rests now.

> * A " host " is a bad cough.

CROFTON HACKETT, WORC.

Here lieth the body of John Guley, Senr. in expectation of the last day. What sort of a man he was that Day will discover. He was Clerk of this Parish 55 years. He died in 1756, aged 75.

N.B.—This dubious remark occurs also at Ilfracombe, and in other churchyards.

WILBRAHAM, CAMB.

May this monument be sustained
To the end of Time
Sacred
to the Memory and Virtues of
Miss Mary Ward
the darling of her friends
the admiration of strangers
and real blessing of her family.
Her person
was tall and graceful
Her features
Handsome and regular
but her mind
Pious, Modest, Delicate, and Amiable
beyond the credit of description
Parents of children
and inhabitants of her native village
drop a tear
to this sweet short-lived flower
Who having just added a complete education
to her natural excellencies
Died
Uncommonly Perfect and Lamented
on the 30th Jan. of
1756
Aged 15 years 6 months.

BAKEWELL, DERBY.

> Know posterity that on the 8th of April in the
> year of Grace 1757 the rambling remains of the
> above said John Dale were in the 86th year of his
> pilgrimage, laid upon his two wives.

> This thing, in life might cause some jealousy :
> Here all three lie together lovingly :
> But from embraces here no pleasure flows,
> Alike are here all human joys and woes.
> Here Sarah's chiding John no longer hears,
> And old John's rambling Sarah no more fears :
> A period's come to all their toilsome lives :
> The Goodman's quiet, still are both his wives.

1757.   *John Dale*

NEWNHAM, GLOS.

> From every blusterous storm of life,
> And that worst storm, domestic strife,
> Which shipwrecked all our social joys,
> And every worldly bliss destroys :
> I luck'ly am arrived at last,
> And safe in port my anchor's cast ;
> Where sheltered by the blissful shore
> Nought shall disturb, or vex me more :
> But joys serene, and calmest peace
> Which Christ bestows, shall never cease.

1759.   *Thomas Yerbury.*

ALMONDSBURY, GLOS.

> The costly marble may perhaps express
> In lying lines th' Unworthy's worthiness :
> My humble stone shall this sad truth convey,
> The best beloved is soonest call'd away.
> Full short, but full of honour, was thy span,
> Thou tender Husband, and thou Honest Man.

1760.   *Benjamin Dobins.*

RIPON, YORKS.

> Here lieth John James
> Cook of Newby
> who was a faithful servant to his master
> and an
> upright downright honest man

> Bones among stones
> Do lie full still :
> While the soul wanders
> E'en where God will.

1760.   John Cook.

BARNWELL PRIORY CHURCH.

> Man's life is but a winter's day
> Some only breakfast and away
> Others to dinner stay and are full fed
> The oldest man but sups and goes to bed
> Long is his life who lingers out the day
> Who goes the soonest has the least to pay.

1772.   John Stewart.

There are many variations on this theme.

SELBY ABBEY.

> Beneath this stone lies Archer John
> Late Sexton I aver
> Who without tears for 34 years
> Did carcasses inter,
> Till to his dismay, on a Summer day,
> Death to him once did say—
> Leave off your trade, be not afraid
> But follow me away.
> Without reply, or word or sigh,
> The Summons he obey'd :
> In seventeen hundred and fifty eight
> Resigned his life and spade.

1758.   John Archer, aged 74.

LLANBELIG, CARN.

> " Of such is the kingdom of Heaven."

> Here lie the remains of Thomas Chambers
> Dancing Master
> whose genteel address and assiduity
> in Teaching
> recommended him to all that had the
> pleasure of his acquaintance
> He died June 13, 1765
> Aged 31.

GUILDSPELD, MONTG.

> Under this Yew tree
> Buried he would be
> Because his father he
> Planted this Yew tree.

> 1769. *David Williams.*

RIPON, YORKS.

> Short was my stay in this vain world,
> All but a seeming laughter,
> Therefore mark well my words and ways
> For thou com'st posting after.

> 1770. *Jane Shepherd.*

STOKE, SURREY.

> More would you have ? Go ask the poor he fed
> Whose was the hand that raised their drooping head :
> Ask of the few whose path is strewn with flowers
> Who made the happy still have happier hours :
> Whose voice like his could charm all care away,
> Whose look so tender, or whose smile so gay :
> Go ask of all—and learn from every tear
> The good how honoured, and the kind how dear.

> 1800. *William Aldersley.*

LOWESTOFT, SUFFOLK.

In memory of
Charles Ward
who died May 1770
aged 63 years
a dutiful son, a loving brother
And an affectionate husband.

N.B. This stone was not erected by *Susan* his wife.
She erected a stone to John Salter, her *second* husband,
forgetting the affection of Charles Ward, her first
husband.

Let no one disturb his bones.

NEWLAND, GLOS.

Say more I need not, and say less who can,
Here lies the generous, humane, honest man.

1770. *George Morgan.*

HANTLEP, ESSEX.

I coo and pine and ne'er shall be at rest
Till I come to the Dearest, Sweetest, Best

Rebeka Gregor
daughter of John Osborne Esqr.
of this Parish lies here buried.

1771.

ST. PHILIP'S, BIRMINGHAM.

O cruel Death, how could you be so unkind,
To take him before and leave me behind ?
You should have taken both of us if either,
Which would have been more pleasing to the survivor.

1781. *James Barker.*

E

Ercall Magna, Salop.

When terrestial all in chaos shall exhibit effervesence
Then celestial virtues with their full effulgent brilliant
essence
Shall with beaming beauteous radiance through the
ebullition shine
Transcending to glorious regions beautiful sublime :
Then human power absorbed, deficient to delineate such
effulgent lasting sparks,
Where honest plebeians ever will have precedence over
ambiguous great Monarchs

1779. *Richard and Elizabeth Barklamb.*

Kirk St. Anne, I. of Man.

Here, friend, is little Daniel's tomb,
To Joseph's age he did arrive ;
Sloth killing thousands in their bloom
While labour kept poor Dan alive.
Tho' strange, yet true, full seventy years
Was his wife happy in her tears.

Daniel Tear, died Dec. 9, 1787, aged 110 years.

Harborne, nr. Birmingham.

O cruel death, so soon to end
Two faithful wives and sincere friends
Death takes the good, too good on earth to stay
And leaves the bad, too bad to take away.

Ripon, Yorks.

Here lies poor but honest
Bryan Tunstall
He was a most expert angler
until Death, envious of his mart
threw out his line, hooked him
and
landed him here the 21st day of April
1790.

EVERTON, LANC.

Here lie
the earthly remains of
John Berridge
late Vicar of Everton
And an itinerant servant of Jesus Christ
who loved his Master and his work
and after running on his errands many years
was caught up to wait on Him in Heaven

Reader
Art thou born again
No salvation without a new birth

I was born in sin February 1716
Remained ignorant of my fallen state till 1730
Lived proudly on faith and works for
Salvation till 1754

Admitted to Everton Vicarage, 1755 :
Fled to Jesus alone for refuge, 1756 :
Fell asleep in Jesus January 22, 1793.

Rev. John Berridge.

(Written by himself except the last date).

KNARESDELL, NORTH.

All you that please these lines to read,
It will cause a tender heart to bleed.
I was murdered upon this fell,
And by a man I knew full well.
By bread and butter which he laid
I, being harmless, was betrayed.
I hope he will rewarded be
That laid the poison there for me.

1796. *Robert Baxter*

TEWKESBURY, WORC.

Here lies the only comfort of
My life, who was the best of
Husbands to a wife, since
he is not, no joy I e'er shall
have Till laid by him
within the silent grave :
Here we shall sleep, and quietly
remain, Till by God's decree
we meet in Heaven again.
There with Christ eternally
to dwell, And until that
blest time, my Love, Farewell.

1800. *John Hart, the 6th descendant from Shakespeare.*

CHIPPING SODBURY, GLOS.

Here is the wardrobe of my dusty clothes
Which hands divine shall brush, and make so gay
That my immortal soul shall put them on
And wear the same upon my Wedding day.
In which attire my Lord shall me convoy
Then to the lodging of eternal joy.

1642. *Elizabeth Oldfield.*

GT. WALFORD, WORC.

Here old John Randall lies
Who counting from his tale
Lived three score years and ten
Such virtue was in Ale.
Ale was his meat,
Ale was his drink
Ale did his heart revive :
And if he could have drunk his Ale
He still had been alive :
But he died January five

1699 *John Randall.*

The same epitaph is said also to be in Walford Magna
Churchyard, Warwick.

MASHAM, YORKS.

Another acrostic epitaph—Christopher Kay.

Confined in a bed of dust
Here doth a body lie
Raised again it will be I trust
Into the heavens high
Sin not but have a care
To make your calling sure
Omit those things which trivial are
Prize that which will endure
Hang not your mind on secular things
Each one doth fade apace
Riches the chief of which hath wings

Keeping no certain place
Addict yourselves unto his conversation
You purchase heaven for your habitation.

1689.   Christopher Kay.

BRIDGE SOLERS, HEREFORD.

Lo here he lies ! His poor remains
This gloomy monument contains :
Let fame in happy story tell
How much he others did excel
In living and in loving well.
Blest with a competent estate,
None thought him little, none too great.
From pride and avarice exempt
Unenvied yet above contempt.
To those in want Heaven's almoner
To all his friends extremely dear
Sincerely loyal to his Prince,
A favourite of Providence.
Oh had I lived a life like thine
I then might wish this grave were mine.

1698.   John Geers, aged 80.

LANGFORD, BERKS.

Within this Little House three houses lie
John Howse, James Howse, the short-liv'd twins, and I
Anne, of John Howse once the endeared wife
Who lost mine own to give those babes their life,
We three though dead yet speak and put in mind
The Husband, Father whom we left behind
That we were houses only made of clay,
And called for, could no longer here stay,
But were laid here to take our rest and ease
By Death, who taketh whom and where he please.

1691.

BROUGH, LINC.

The wise—the eloquent—the just
Lies here interred among the dust
Below, who forty years and more
Was Sheriff—now in Heaven's store
How wise and understanding too
At 86 as those that woo—
When Death, with crooked scythe and glass
Set out the bounds he should not pass,
Saintlike his sickness, and his death
Admired by all.   His parting breath
So sweet as might perfume the earth
Doubtless that spotless soul of his
Is gone into eternal bliss.

1690.   *Thomas Gabetis, Steward to the Countess of Pembroke.*

ARBROATH, N.B.

Here lies a wife was chaste, a mother blest,
A modest woman, all these in one chest!
Sarah unto her mate, Mary to God
Martha unto men, whilst here she had abode.

1699.   *Grisell West.*

CARRY, BY EDINBURGH.

> Beneath these stones lie Meekie's bones ;
> Oh ! Satan gin ye take him,
> Appoint him tutor to your weans
> And clever deils he mak'em.
>
> *Andrew Meekie, late parish dominie.*

ELGIN CATHEDRAL.

Here is the burial place appointed for John Geedes, Glover, Burgess in Elgin, and Isobell McKean his spouse, and their relations.

> Grace me good : in hope I bide.

> This world is a city
> full of streets, and
> Death the merchant
> that all men meets.
> If life were a thing
> that money could buy,
> The poor could not live
> and the rich
> would not die.
>
> 1689.

Versions of this epitaph are also found in Kent and Herts.

EAST HORNDEN, ESSEX.

> Could this stone speak it would the reader tell
> She that lies here did her whole sex excel :
> And why should death with a promiscuous hand
> In one rude stroke impoverish a land.
>
> 1690. *Martha Tyrrell.*

STRATHMARTEN, N.B.

> Among the earth beneath this stone
> Doth his forefathers lie
> And this hath been their burial place
> Since mans rememberie.
>
> 1690. *James Anderson.*

Whitmarsh, Warwick.

The first of the two following epitaphs was on the Rev. Nicholas Greenhill, first Headmaster of Rugby School, who died in 1650, aged 70. It was written and set up 39 years after his decease by the Rev. R. Boles, his successor in the Rectory of Whitmarsh who also composed for himself the second epitaph, which appears on a brass plate near the other.

> This Greenhill periwig'd with snow
>   Was levelled in the Spring :
> This Hiss the Nine and Three did know
>   Was sacred to his King
> But he must Down although so much Divine
> Before he rises never to set but shine.

> This mirror makes me slight a life half dead,
> Because a better comes when this is fled.
> My time and place where I do live are known :
> My death and grave none knows but God alone.
> My death is certain, and uncertain, then
> Mortals beware, Death comes you know not when.
> I value not a tomb, obscure to lie
> With virtue is our immortality
> My life runs on five years before four score
> Once I must die and then shall die no more.

1689.

North Mimms, Herts.

> Thus youth, and age, and all things pass away,
> Thy turn is now as his was yesterday :
> Tomorrow shall another take thy room,
> The next day he a prey for worms become :
> And on your dusty bones shall others tread,
> As now you walk and trample on the dead,
> Till neither sign or memory appear,
> That you had ever birth or being here.

STANFORD, NOTTS.

> Here lies the body of Mr. Francis, the son of
> Mr. Francis Thwaits, Rector of Stanford and
> of Ann his wife, who died the 4th of September
> in the second year of his age. 1700.

> No careful nurses
> To their bed do lay
> Their children which too
> Long would wanton play :
> So to prevent all my
>   Ivening crimes,
> Nature my nurse laid
> Me to bed betimes.

Many of the old London Churches were destroyed
in the Great Fire, but several of the most interesting
epitaphs had already been preserved by John Weever,
who wrote his *Ancient Funeral Monuments* in 1631, and
by John Stone, who made his *Survey of London* in 1598,
and issued a second edition in 1618. Of this collection
of London epitaphs many are taken from these sources.
The spelling has been modernised.

ST. ALBAN'S, WOOD STREET.

> What, is she dead ? doth he survive ?
> No, both are dead, and both alive.
> She lives, he's dead, by love, thro' grieving
> In him, for her, yet dead, yet living.
> Both dead and living ? then what is gone ?
> One half of both, not any one.

> One Mind, one Faith, one Hope, one Grace
> In Life, in Death, they had, and still they have.
> 1611. *Anne Gibson.*

St. Matthew's, Friday Street.

> As man liveth, so he dieth
> As tree falleth, so it lieth
> Anne Middleton, thy life well past
> Doth argue restful bliss at last.

> 1596.

In St. John Zachary, one of the City Churches not rebuilt after the great Fire, there was an epitaph on Sir James Pemberton, died 1613, which took the form of a dialogue between Virtue and Death.

> Virtue and Death being both enamoured
> on worthy *Pemberton* in heat of love
> To be possessed of what each coveted
> Thus did they dialogue, and thus they strove.

Virtue.	What Virtue challengeth, is but her right.
Death.	What Death lays claim to, who can contradict ?
V.	Virtue whose power exceeds all other might.
D.	Where's Virtue's power when Death makes all submit ?
V.	I gave him life, and therefore he is mine.
D.	That life he held no longer than I list.
V.	I made him more than mortal, near Divine.
D.	How hapt he could not then Death's stroke resist ?
V.	Because (by nature) all are born to die.
D.	Then thine own tongue yields Death the victory.
V.	No, Death, thou are deceived, thy envious stroke Hath given him life immortal, 'gainst thy will.
D.	What life can be but vanisheth as smoke ?
V.	A life that all thy darts can never kill.
D.	Have I not locked his body in the grave ?
V.	That was but dust, and that I bid thee keep.
D.	That is as much as I desire to have His comely shape in my eternal sleep.
V.	But where's his honourable life, renown, and fame.

D.   They are but breath, them I resign to thee.
V.   Them most I covet.   D. I prefer my claim
         His body mine.   V. Mine is Eternity.

And so they ceased. Death triumph's o'er his grave
Virtue o'er that which Death can never have.

ST. ANDREW'S, HOLBORN.

My Turtle gone, all joy is gone from me
I'll mourn awhile, and after flee :
For time brings youthful Youths to age
And Age brings Death, our heritage.

They lived married together 44 years
Their race is run, and Heaven is won.

1603. *Richard Aldworth and Elizabeth his wife.*

ST. LEONARD'S, SHOREDITCH.

Her corpse here lies in chest
Her soul in Heaven now lives,
And she enjoys that rest
Which God to his saints gives
For in Christ did she trust,
That he will her restore
Again out of the dust
To live for evermore.

1592. *Elizabeth, Widow of John Skory, Bishop of Hereford.*

ST. STEPHEN, COLEMAN STREET.

If human worth could have preserved him still,
He had been much too strong for death to kill
Yet being conquered, he got, by the strife,
A better being in a better life :
So that great victor over nature left him
More happiness tenfold than he bereft him.

1611. *Barne Roberts.*

ALL HALLOWS, LOMBARD STREET.

The soul in Heaven, the body here, of Izan lies
By her John Edwards good, and by her parents both :
She dear to all her three, that living, still she cries
Lay me by them, for other grave I loathe
Oh God ! that heardst the cry of this thy creature
Make Izans many, in Virtue, Grace, and Feature.

> As love (in life) conjoined us once,
> And God (by death) disjoined us twain :
> So love (by death) rejoined our bones
> And God (in joy) joined us again.
>
> 1613.   *Izan Edwards.*

ST. MARGARET, LOTHBURY.

> The blessed token of the Daughter's love
> Unto the Father's kind and loving care,
> May to the World this Monument approve,
> How blessed Parents in their children are :
>   And blessed God, that so his love expresseth
>   Who thus both Parents and the Children blesseth.
>
> 1620.   *John and Berseba Taylor.*

ST. SAVIOUR'S, SOUTHWARK.

There is some comfort for grocers in this epitaph.

> Some called him Garret, but that was too high,
> His name was Jarret that here doth lie :
> Who in his life was tost on many a wave,
> And now he lies anchored in his own grave.
> The Church he did frequent while he had breath
> He desired to lie therein after his death.
> To heaven he is gone, the way before
> Where of Grocers there is many more.
>
> 1626.   *John Jarret.*

St. Pancrate, Needler's Lane.

Here lies a Mary, mirror of her sex
For all that best their souls and bodies decks
Faith, form or fame, the miracle of youth,
For zeal and knowledge of the sacred Truth,
For frequent reading the whole Holy Writ,
For fervent prayer, and for practise fit,
For meditations, full of use and art,
For humbleness in habit and in heart,
For pious, prudent, peaceful, praiseful life,
For all the virtues of a Christian wife :
For patient bearing, seven dead-bearing throws
For one alive, which yet dead with her goes.

From *Travers* her dear spouse, her father *Hayes*
Lord Mayor, more honoured in her virtuous praise.
1614. *Mary Travers.*

An epitaph in St Botolph's, Aldersgate, not only describes a " paragon of virtues," but also claims that they were the result of good family breeding.

What epitaph shall we afford this shrine ?
Words cannot grace this Pyramid of thine :
Thy sweet perfections, all summed up, were such
As heaven (I think) for faith did think too much
Religious zeal did thy pure heart command
Pity thine eye, and Charity thy hand :
These graces, joined with more of like degree
Make each man's word an Epitaph for thee
Calm was thy death, well-ordered was thy life
A careful mother, and a loving wife.
Ask any, how these virtues in thee grew ?
Thou wast a Spencer and a Montague.
1612. *Catherine Montague.*

ST. SWITHIN, CANNON STREET.

He possessed earth as he might Heaven possess
Wise to do right, but never to oppress
His charity was better felt than known,
For when he gave there was no trumpet blown
What can more be comprised in one man's fame,
To crown a soul, and leave a living name.

1632.   *George Bolles, Lord Mayor.*

ALL HALLOWS, BREAD STREET.

Thy lifeless Trunk
(O Reverend Stock)
Like Aaron's rod
Sprouts out again :
And after two
Full winters past
Yields Blossomes
And ripe fruit amain.
For why, this work of piety
Performed by some of thy Flock
To thy dead corpse and sacred urn
Is but the fruit of this old Stock.

1628.   *Rev. Richard Stock.*

BUNHILL FIELDS CEMETERY.

Dear Holmes hath found
A Home among the blest,
His wearied body for to rest :
For nowhere can his Flesh
True slumber have,
But in this truest Home in Homely grave
His soul in Heavenly tunes doth sing
   Hell, where's thy Triumph ?
   Death, where's thy Sting ?

1694.   *Thomas Holmes.*

St. Dunstan's in the West.

> Here Edward Cordell, Squire, lies :
> Who, when he life possessed,
> Had place among the learned and wise
> And credit with the best.
> *Abigail Henningham*, his wife
> This monument prepared,
> For love to him, who in his life,
> To love her well declared.
> God hath his soul, this earth his earth,
> Her heart his love still keeps,
> The odds 'twixt you and him is breath,
> Which gone, all flesh thus sleeps.
>
> 1631. *Edward Cordell.*

St. Bartholomew's.

> Within this hollow vault there rests the frame
> Of the high Soul which once informed the same :
> Torn from the service of the State in's prime
> By a disease malignant as the time :
> Whose life and death designed no other end
> Than to serve God, his Country, and his Friend :
> Who when Ambition, Tyranny, and Pride
> Conquered the Age, conquered himself and died.
>
> 1641. *James Rivers.*

St. Helen's, Bishopsgate.

Epitaph
on the lamented death of his honoured friend
William Drax,
Esq., who exchanged this life for immortality Decem. 17,
1669, in the 63 year of his age.

> To thy dear memory blest soul I pay
> This humble tribute though in such a way
> As rather doth proclaim my want of skill
> Than any want of love or heart or will

True to thy trust none in thy memory
Can change thee more or less with treachery
Bring forth the person, Rich, poor, old or young
That can justly say he ever did them wrong
In others weal or woe thy heart
Would sympathise and take its part
Oh what's more like the Deity
Than blessed hoary piety
A soul fitted for heaven when glorious Grace
Triumphs with him in his sure resting place
But is he dead?   Can I believe
That he should die and we should live
Methinks we may the knot untie
Better to live fitter to die
Now death I see doth wisely choose
The gold but doth the dross refuse
Sleep not without hope cry not alas
He's better where he is than where he was
Hark, is not that his voice doth he not say
Heaven's meanest mansion, is worth this globe of clay
Who so doth live and do and die like thee
His fame shall last to all eternity.

STEPNEY.

An epitaph which with slight variations is used on the
tombs of seafaring men is the following.   It is also found
at Ipswich, Ilfracombe, and other places.

> Though Boreas' blasts and Neptune waves
>   Have tossed me to and fro :
> In spite of both by Heaven's decree,
>   Harbour I here below.
> Where I do now at anchor ride
>   With many of our fleet :
> Yet once again I must set sail
> Our Admiral Christ to meet.

1697.   *Captain John Dunch.*

At St. Michael's, Eastcheap, is a memorial to Robert Preston, late drawer at the " Boar's Head Tavern," Great Eastcheap, aged 27, who died in 1730.

> Bacchus, to give the toping world surprise
> Produced one sober son, and here he lies.
> Tho' nursed among full hogsheads, he defied
> The charm of wine, and every vice beside.
> O reader, if to justice thou'rt inclined,
> Keep honest Preston daily in thy mind.
> He drew good wine, took care to fill his pots,
> Had sundry virtues that outweighed his faults.
> You that on Bacchus have the like dependence,
> Pray copy Bob in measure of attendance.

St. Pancras Churchyard.

> Underneath this stone doth lie
> The body of Mr. Humpherie
> Jones, who was of late
> By trade a plate
> Worker in Barbicanne ;
> Well known to be a good man
> By all his friends and neighbours too,
> And paid everybody their due.
> He died in the year 1737
> August 10th, aged 80 ; his soul we hope's in heaven.

St. Pancras.

> Go spotless Honour and unsullied Truth
> Go smiling Innocence and blooming Youth,
> Go female Sweetness, joined with manly Sense,
> Go winning Wit that never gave offence.
> Go lost Humanity that blest the poor,
> Go faint-eyed Patience from affliction's door,
> Go Modesty that never wore a frown,
> Go Virtue and receive thy heavenly Crown.

Not from a stranger came this heartfelt verse,
The Friend inscribed thy Tomb, whose Tears bedewed thy
hearse. 1756. *Miss Bassett.*

F

Arreton, Isle of Wight.

The writer of this epitaph having married for the third time thought it a fitting occasion to erect a monument to his two former spouses. The first having had fifteen children, and the second being childless he finds virtues in both.

To the remembrance of the two most worthy and religious Gentlewomen, his late dear and loyal wives, Mrs. Elizabeth Bamfield, who died 7th March 1615, having been the mother of 15 hopeful children. And Mrs. Gertrude Parceval who died childless the 22nd December 1619 was this monument consecrated by their loving and sorrowful husband Barnabas Leigh.

Since neither pen nor pencil can set forth
Of these two matchless wives the matchless worth,
W'are forced to cover in this silent tomb
The prayers of a chaste and fruitful womb.
And with Death's sable veil in darkness hide
The rich rare virtues of a barren bride.
Sweet saint-like pair of souls on whom did shine
Such models of perfection feminine.
Such piety, love, zeal, that tho' we sinners
Their lives have lost ; yet still themselves are winners.
For they, secure, Heaven's happiness inherit,
While we lament their loss, admire their merit.

1619.   *Elizabeth and Gertrude Leigh.*

St. Giles', Norwich.

My name speaks what I was and am, and have,
A Bedding field, a piece of earth, a grave :
Where I expect until my soul doth wing
Unto the field an everlasting spring.
For raise and raise out of the earth and slime
God did the first and will the second time.

1637.   *Elizabeth Bedingfield.*

ANCIENT EPITAPHS

73

CARISBROOKE, ISLE OF WIGHT.

Here lieth the body of the right worthy Wm. Keeling, Esquire, Groom of the Chamber to our Sovereign Lord King James, General for the Hon. East India Adventures, where he was thrice employed, and dieing on this isle at the age of 42, 1619. Sept. 12th hath this remembrance been fixed by his loving and sorrowful wife Anne Keeling.

Forty and two years on this vessel frail
On the rough seas of Life did Keeling sail
A Merchant fortunate, a Captain bold,
A Courtier gracious, yet alas ! not old.
Such Worth, Experience, Honour, and High praise,
Few win in twice so many years and days.
But what the world admired, he deemed but dross
For Christ : without Christ all his gain but loss,
For him and his dear love, with merry cheer
To the Holy Land his last course he did steer.
Faith served for sails, the Sacred Word for Cord,
Hope was his anchor, Glory his reward.
And thus with Gales of Grace, by happy venture
Through Straits of Death, Heaven's harbour he did enter.

HADLEIGH, SUFFOLK.

The Charnel mounted in the W
Sits to be seen in Funer
A Matron plain, Domestic
In care and pains Continu
Not slow, not gay, nor prodig
Yet neighbourly and hospit
Her children seven yet living
Her 61st year hence did C
To rest her body natur
In hope to rise spiritu

ALL

1630. *Ellen Keson.*

Bakenham, Suffolk.

It will be noticed that this epitaph is an acrostic. The name is Richard Swift.

> Reader know that this narrow earth
> Incaseth one whose name and worth
> Can live when marble turns to dust :
> Honour'd abroad for wise and just
> Ask the Russ and Sweden, these
> Report his prudence with their pence.
> Dear when at home, to his faith given,
> Steadfast as earth, devote to Heaven.
> Wise merchant he some storms endured
> In the best port his soul secured
> For fear thou should'st forget his name
> Tis the first Epitaph of fame.

1620. Richard Swift.

Blatherwycke, Northants.

Here sleep thirteen together in one tomb,
And all these great, yet quarrel not for room,
The muses and the graces here did meet,
And graved these letters on the churlish sheet ·
Who, having wept their fountains dry,
Through the conduit of the eye,
For the friend who here doth lie
Crept into his grave and died,
And so the riddle is untied,
For which this Church, prove that the fates bequeath
Unto her ever honoured trust,
So much and that so precious dust,
Hath twined her temples with an ivy wreath,
Which should have laurel been,
But that the grieved plant, to see him dead,
      Took pet and withered.

1635. Thomas Randolph. Poet.

Lindridge, Worcester.

> This stone that covers earth and clay
> Long in the earth uncovered lay :
> Man forced it from the mother's womb
> And made thereof for man a tomb.
> And now it speaks and thus doth say
> The life of man is but a day :
> The days will pass, the night must come :
> Then here, poor man, is all thy room
> The writer and the reader must
> Like this good man be turned to dust :
> He lived well, and so do thou :
> Then fear not death, when, where or how
> It comes : 'twill end all grief and pain
> And make thee ever live again.

1623. *William Penell.*

Geddington, Northants.

An epitaph on a bachelor. Notice the reference to freedom from wedlock, care, or strife.

> If, Who lies here ? thou dost enquire,
> Read, and so have thy desire.
> Richard Best, his name and free
> Of the Haberdasher's Company.
> The privilege of Merchants he
> Did claim with the like liberty
> The years that here he passed o'er
> Wanted by one of four score.
> Forty years he abroad did toil
> The rest he spent on his own soil.
> Free from wedlock, care or strife,
> He wedded was to single life
> To have more spoke he did deserve
> But 'twas his will that this should serve.

He died the 29th *April,* 1629.

BURFORD, OXON.

Here shadows lie
Whilst earth is sad :
Still hopes to die
To him she had.

So shall I be
With him I loved :
And him with me
And both as blessed.

In bliss is he
Whom I loved best ;
Thrice happy she
With him to rest

Love made me poet
And this I writ :
My heart did do it
And not my wit.

1625.   *Sir Lawrence Tanfield (written by his wife).*

KENDAL, WESTMORELAND.

London bred me   — Westminster fed me
Cambridge sped me   — My sister wed me
Study taught me   — living sought me
Learning brought me — Kendal caught me
Labour pressed me   — sickness distressed me
Death oppressed me   — the grave possessed me
God first gave me   — Christ did save me
Earth did crave me   — and—heaven would have me.

1627.   *Rev. Ralph Fyer.*

ONIBURY, SALOP.

Here lies, divorced from her husband's side,
One that by death is made her Saviour's bride ;
For on Good-Friday He did her betroth
Unto himself for ever where he goeth
And thus united she a guest became
Unto the Marriage Supper of the Lamb.
Leaving her earthly mate grief to sustain
Till death, by striking him, weds her again.
O languish then, my soul until I see
My dearest wife in her felicity.

1630.   *Dorothy Pytt.*

DAGENHAM, ESSEX.

> Were here no epitaph or monument,
> Nor line nor marble to declare the intent
> Yet goodness hath a lashing memory,
> The just are like to Kings that never die.
> Then Death a passage or translation is,
> An end of woes, an orient to Bliss.
> Thrice happy couple that do now possess
> The fruits of thine good works and holiness,
> Now God rewards their alms and charity
> Their strict observance of Sabaoth's piety.
> Here were they wont to spend their seventh day,
> Here was their love, their life, their Heaven's way.
> Here did they pray, but now they praises sing.
>
> And God accepts their souls sweet offering,
> Only their bodies here remain in ground,
> Waiting the surge of the last Trumpet's sound.

> 1627-8. *James Hardy and Elizabeth his wife.*

WHITWELL, DERBY.

In memory of the Right Noble, Learned and Religious Knight, Rogers Manners of Whitwell, in the County of Derby, who died the 17th July A.D. 1632.

> A living Academy was this Knight
> Divinity, the arts, the tongues, what might
> In learned schools exactly, he professed
> Took up their lodging in his Noble breast
> Till Death like Church destroyers did pull down
> *Manners*, true fabric and the arts renown.

CONWAY.

Here lieth the body of Nick Hookes, of Conway, Gent, who was the forty-first child of his father William Hookes, Esqre. by Alice his Wife, & the father of 27 children, who died the 20th day of March, 1637.

CHELTENHAM, GLOS.

> Dear souls & blest ! you both delivered be,
> Having exchanged your prisons before me :
> Whilst I survive to live, and found it true
> That I grieve for myself more than for you.
> Nor can tears quench my zeal, like funeral fire
> That flames for her I loved till I expire.

> 1640. *The wife and daughter of Dr. English, Vicar.*

GREY MAIS, EDINBURGH.

> To-day is mine, to-morrow yours may be :
> Each mortal man should mind that he must die.
> What is man's life ? A shade, a smoke, a flower.
> Short to the good, to the bad doth long endure.

> If thou list that passeth by,
> Know whom in this Tomb doth lie.
> Thomas Bannatine, abroad
> And or home who served God,
> Though no children he possessed,
> Yet the Lord with means him blest,
> He on them did well dispose,
> Long ere death his eyes did close,
> For the poor his helping hand
> And his friends his kindness found ;
> And on his dear bedfellow
> Janet McMath he did bestow,
> Out of his lovely affection,
> A fit and goodly portion.
> Thankful she herself to prove,
> For a sign of mutual love,
> Did no pains nor charges spare
> To set up this fabric rare ;
> As Artemise, that noble dame.
> To her dear Mausolus' name.

> 1635. *Thomas Bannatine.*

IGHTHAM, KENT.

This lady is traditionally said to have written the letter which led to the discovery of the " Gunpowder plot," The reference is to her needlework, specimens of which were suspended over her tomb.

She was a Dorcas
Whose curious needle wound the abused stage
Of this lewd world into the golden age,
Whose pen of steel and silken ink enrolled
The acts of Jonah in records of gold.
Whose art disclosed that plot, which, had it taken,
Rome had triumphed and Britain's walls been shaken.

She was
In heart a Lydia, and in tongue a Hannah,
In zeal a Ruth, in wedlock a Susanna
Prudently simple, providently wary,
To the world a Martha, and to Heaven a Mary.

Who put on } in the year of { Pilgrimage 69
immortality } her { Redeemer 1641

Dame Dorothy Selby.

ST. MICHAEL'S IN THE HAMLET, LIVERPOOL.
Venus in Sole Visa Nov. 24, 1639.

In Memory of
Jeremiah Horrox, One of the Greatest
Astronomers this Kingdom ever produced.
Born in Toxteth Park in 1619
Died in 1641. Aged 22.

His observations were made at Hoole
Eight miles from Preston, where he
Predicted, and was the First Person
Who saw the Transit of Venus
Over the Sun

GREAT WILLASTON, CHESHIRE.

The Old, Old, very Old man, Thomas Parr, was born at the Glyn within This Chapelry of Great Willaston and Parish of Alberbury, in the county of Salop. In the Year of our Lord 1483. He lived in the Reigns of Ten Kings and Queens of England (viz) K. Edw. 4, K. Edw. 5, K. Rich. 3, K. Hen. 7, K. Hen. 8, K. Edw. 6, Q. Mary, Q. Eliz., K. James 1, and K. Charles 1; died the 13th and was buried in Westminster Abbey on the 15th of November 1635. Aged 152 years and nine months.

WING, BUCKS.

> Honest old Thomes Cotes, that sometimes was
> Porter at Ascott Hall, hath now (alas !)
> Left his key, lodge, fire, friends, and all, to have
> A rocm in Heaven.   This is that good man's grave
> Reader prepare for thine, for none can tell
> But that you two may meet to-night.   Farewell.

He died the 20th of   Set up at the appointment
November, 1648.   & charges of his friend

Geo. Houghton.

BANBURY, OXON.

To the memory of Mr. William Whateley, later Alderman and once Mayor of this borough.   Died Jan. 24, 1647.

> He was like Enoch in his walk,
> In zeal like Phineas more than talk :
> Job-like a perfect upright man,
> In mercy the Samaritan.
> A foe to error and false ways
> A strict observer of God's days.
> Call up the account, and when you're done
> Say, we have lost many in one.

Eᴀꜱᴛ Bᴇʀɢʜᴏʟᴛ, Sᴜꜰꜰᴏʟᴋ.

Here is an unusual alliterative epitaph.

Edward		
Ever	Edward Lambe	Lambe
Envied	Second son of	Lived
Evil	Thomas Lambe	Laudably
Endured	of Trimley	Lord
Extremities	Esquire	Let
Even	all his days	Like
Earnestly	he lived a Bachelor	Life
Expecting	well learned in Divine	Learn
Eternal	and Common Laws	Ledede
Ease	with his counsel he	Livers
	helped many, yet took	Lament
	fees scarce of any	

He died the 19*th of November,* 1647.

Cʜɪᴄʜᴇʟᴇʏ, Oxᴏɴ.

Grieved at the world and crimes, this early bloom
Looked round, and sighed, and stole into his tomb,
His fall was like his birth, too quick this rose
Made haste to spread, and the same haste to close.
Here lies his dust, but his best tomb's fled hence
For marble cannot last like innocence.

1640. *John Chester, aged* 3 *years.*

Aᴠᴇʀʜᴀᴍ, Nᴏᴛᴛꜱ.

Sir William Sutton corpse here tombed sleeps,
Whose happy soul in better mansions keeps ;
These nine years lived he with his lady fair
A lovely, noble and like virtuous pair.
Their generous offspring (parents joy of heart)
Eight of each sex : of each an equal part,
Ushered to Heaven their father, the other
Remain'd behind him to attend their mother.

1640. *Sir Wm. Sutton.*

CALBOURNE, ISLE OF WIGHT.

Here is another of those anagram epitaphs in which the effect is, as usual, much strained.

> Blest is the just man's memory
> Both here and in eternity.
> Being dead he yet speaketh
> Heb. XX. IIV.

> In memory of the Reverend Religious and learned Preacher
> Daniel Evance
> Who was born at London, March 2, 1613,
> and died at Calbourne, December 27, 1652.

This monument was erected by Hannah, his mournful relict. Daniel Evance—Anagram—" I can deal even."

> Who is sufficient for this thing
> Wisely to harp on every string
> Rightly divide the word of truth
> To babes and men, to age & youth ?
> One of a thousand—where's he found,
> So learned, pious, and profound ?
> Earth has but few—there is in heaven
> One who answers—" I can deal even."
>
> 1652.   *Daniel Evance.*

HUNSTANTON, NORFOLK.

> In Heaven at home, a blessed change
> Who while I was on earth was Strange.
>
> 1654.   *Hamon de Strange.*

GREAT MILTON, OXON.

> Here lie mother and babe both without sins
> Next birth will make her and her infant twins.
>
> 1654.   *The wife of Dr. H. Wilkinson.*

Stratford-on-Avon.

The epitaph to Shakespeare's daughter. It will be noted that Shakespeare is spelt in two different ways.

Here lieth the body of Susanna, wife to John Hall, gent: the daughter of Mr. William Shakespeare, gent: She deceased the 11th of July A° 1649. Aged 66.

Witty above her sex, but that's not all,
Wise to Salvation was good Mistress Hall:
Something of Shakspeare was in that, but this
Wholly of him unto whom she's now in bliss.

Then, passenger, hast ne'er a tear
 To weep with her that wept with all:
That wept, but set herself to cheer
 Them up, with comforts cordial.
Her love shall live, her mercy spread,
 When thou has ne'er a tear to shed.

Banbury, Oxon.

To the memory of Ric. Richards, who by Gangrene lost first a toe, afterwards a leg, and lastly his life on the 7th day of April, 1656.

Ah! cruel Death to make three meals gone
 To taste and taste till all was gone.
But know, thou Tyrant, when the trump shall call
He'll find his feet and stand where thou shalt fall.

Thurbridge, Essex.

Roger lies here before his hour
Thus doth gardener lose his flower.

1658. *Roger Gardener and wife.*

PRITTLEWELL, ESSEX.

Under this stone two precious gems do lie,
Equal in weight, worth, lustre, and sanctity ;
Yet perhaps one of them do excel ;
Which was't who knows ? ask him that knew them well.
By long enjoyment.   If he thus be pressed
He'll pause, then answer ; truly both were best ;
Wer't in my choice that either of the twain
Might be returned to me to enjoy again,
Which should I choose ? Well, since I know not whether,
I'll mourn for the loss of both, but wish for neither.
Yet here's my comfort, herein lies my hope,
The time a coming Cabinets shall ope.
Which are locked fast ; then shall I see
My Jewels to my joy, my Jewels me.

Here lieth the bodies of Mrs. Anna and Mrs. Dorothy
Freeborne, wives of Mr. Samuel Freeborne, who
departed this life, one on the 31st of July 1641, the
other August the 20th 1658, one aged 33 years, the
other 44.

DARRISDEER, DUMFRIES.

Here lies Daniel McMichel, Martyr, shot dead at
Dalveen by Sir John Dalziel for his adhering to the
Word of God, Christ's Kingly Government in his
House, and the Covenanted Work of Reformation
against tyranny, perjury, and prelacy 1685.   Revelation
XI. II.

As Daniel was cast in lion's den.
For praying unto God and not to men
So lions cruelly devoured me
For bearing witness to Truth's testimony
I rest in peace till Jesus rend the cloud
And judge 'twixt me and those who shed my blood.

VANGE, ESSEX.

Reader, put off thy shoes, thou treadest on Holy earth,
Where lies the rarest Phoenix & her only Birth
Whom she survived, O strange, unheard of wonder
But (alas) now dead, those pavements buried under.
Lament her loss, the world grows worse; of her rare brood
There is none left, to breed the like ; she was so good,
Blest Saint ! once mine Equal, O might I now adore thee
My Bliss, my Love, that thou art gone before me
O let thy Cinders warm that Bed of Dust for me
(Thy mournful husband) till I come by thee.

  1659. *Mary Maule and her only son child Charles.*

BALQUHIDDER, N.B.

  Stones weep though eyes were dry :
  Choicest flowers soonest die :
  Their sun oft sets at noon,
  Whose fruit is ripe in June.
  Then tears of joy be thine,
  Since earth must soon resign
  To God what is divine.

    1680. *Isobel Campbell.*

HAMILTON, N.B.

At Hamilton lie the heads of John Parker, James Hamilton,
and Christopher Strang, who suffered at Edinburgh
7th December, 1666.

  Stay passenger, take notice
    What thou reads
  At Edinboro be our bodies
    Here our heads ;
  Our right hands stood at Lanark
    These we want
  Because with them we sware
    The Covenant.

LITTLE BURSTED, ESSEX.

George } Walton { 1663
George }   { 1664

From the same parents both derived one breath
Both at the font received one name
In the same grave united at one death
In parents, name and grave the same.
Heaven soon conducted us, an earthly pair
To that blest heritage where each is fair
Our bodies wait the joyful resurrection, when

Old time shall cease to be
And little infants we
Rise in Christ Jesus perfect men.

BEVERLEY MINSTER, YORK.

Whate'er I did believe, whate'er I taught
Whate'er He did for me who mankind bought,
Whate'er I suffered in the good fight fought,
By Faith, by Word, in Deed, in Heart, in Thought,
Whate'er remains, now I am hither brought.
Resurgam of them all is the full draught :
Who preacheth aught that is not this is naught :
Reader, learn well, but this one truth from me,
Though I be dead, yet still I preach to thee.

ALDENHAM, HERTS.

Death parts the dearest lovers for a while
But makes them mourn who only used to smile.
But after death our unmixed loves shall tie
Eternal knots between my love and I
I Sarah Smith whom thou didst love alone
For thy dear sake have laid this marble stone.

1674. *John Robinson, aged 23.*

LOWESTOFT, SUFFOLK.

A pious, virtuous, blameless, spotless maid
By cruel Death was suddenly betrayed
Of sweetest life. Alas ! a barbarous crime
To crop a flower so sweet, so near the prime.
Cease brinish tears, forbear your grievous moan,
A happy change 'tis, a Celestial Throne
Prepared is ; what comfort doth this give
To pay a debt, to die and yet to live.

1663. Anne Allen.

TEWKESBURY, WORC.

Another anagram epitaph—on Thomas Merrett—a
"barber and surgeon." Note also the play on the name.

Though only stones salute the reader's eye
Here in deep silence precious dust doth lie
Obscurely sleeping in death's mighty store
Mingled with common earth, till time's no more.
Against Death's stubborn laws who does repine
Since so much Merit did his life resign.
Murmurs and tears are useless in the grave
Else he whole volleys at his tomb might have.
Rest here in peace, who like a faithful steward
Repaired the Church, the poor and needy cured.
Eternal mansions do attend the just,
To clothe with immortality their dust—
Tainted, whilst underground, with worms and rust.

1669.

KURSTON, NORFOLK.

Reader stay, and you shall hear
With your eye, who 'tis lies here :
For when stones do silence break
The voice is seen not heard to speak.

1665. Anne Derey.

G

LENBRIDGE, HERTS.

> In so little place doth lie,
> Virtue, goodness, loyalty.
> He who in all relations stood
> And basest times, both true and good.
> 'Tis for no common loss our tears we shed
> Here the best husband, father, friend is laid.
>
> 1666.   *Edward Penell.*

BANHAM, NORFOLK.

> But is Clark dead ?   What dost thou say ?
> His soul's alive—his body here doth lie
> But in a sleep until the Judgment Day
> And live he shall unto Eternity :
> Men say he's dead—I say so too,
> And ere awhile they'll say the same of you.
>
> 1685.   *Robert Clarke, aged* 59.

BARKING, ESSEX.

> Stay here awhile, and his sad state deplore
> Here lies the body of one *Thomas More :*
> His name was *More*, but now it may be said
> He is no more, because that now he's dead
> And in this place doth lie sepulchred.
>
> 1670.   *Thomas More.*

ST. MULLYON, CORNWALL.

> Earth take thine earth : my sin let Satan have it
> The world my goods, my soul my God who gave it ;
> For from these four, Earth, Satan, World, and God,
> My flesh, my sin, my goods, my soul I had.
>
> 1682.   *Rev. Thomas Flavel.*

B<small>RIGHTWELL</small>-B<small>ALDWIN</small>, O<small>XON</small>.

Here is a bet on an epitaph.

> Here lies Stephen Rumbold
> He lived to the age of an hundred and one
> Sanguine and strong
> A hundred to one you don't live so long.
>
> 1687.

F<small>OLKESTONE</small>, K<small>ENT</small>.

This is a much quoted epitaph.

> A house she hath, it's made of such good fashion
> The tenant ne'er shall pay for reparation :
> Nor will the Landlord ever raise the rent,
> Or turn her out of doors for non-payment
> From chimney-money too, this cell is free
> To such a house as this who would not Tenant be.
>
> 1688. *Rebecca Rogers.*

The gravediggers who applied for an increase in wages to meet the increases under the Rents Act reprinted this epitaph and sent it to their employers.

F<small>OWEY</small>, C<small>ORNWALL</small>.

> Near this a rare jewel's set
> Closed up in a cabinet
> Let no sacrilegious hand
> Break through—'tis the strict command
> Of the jeweller : who hath said
> (And 'tis fit he be obeyed)
> I'll require it safe and sound
> Both above and under ground.
>
> 1655. *Mary Courtney*

BRAUNSTON, NORTHANTS.

> 'Tis true I led a single life
> And ne'er was married in my life,
> For of that sex I ne'er had none :
> It is the Lord : his will be done.

William Borrows. 1703.

ST. MARY MAGDALENE, TAUNTON.

Consecrated to the blessed memory of Robert Graye, Esq., and Founder. Aged 65.

> Taunton bore him : London bred him :
> Pity trained him : Virtue led him.
> Earth enrich'd him : Heaven caressed him.
> Taunton blessed him : London blessed him :
> This thankful town ; that mindful city
> Share his piety and his pity
> What he gave, and how he gave it,
> Ask the poor, and you shall have it.
> Gentle reader, Heaven may strike
> Thy tender heart to do the like.
> Now thine eyes have read the story,
> Give him the praise and God the glory.

1635.

ROAD, SOMERSET.

> Here gathered to his Father lies
> An object of our obsequies :
> Who died desired, and lived beloved
> To most well known, by th' bell approved
> His name present may well prevent
> A larger line on's monument
>   Per me Roberton—filium.

1650. *Rev. Nathanial Hellierd.*

St. Ervan, Cornwall.

> Look on this living saint this matchless sum
> So comprehensive a compendium ;
> A learned scholar painful labourer
> A faithful shepherd true ambassador
> An untired watchman and a shining saint
> A burning taper, beauty without paint.
> Bright gem hath left its casket to be set
> By God unto a nobler coronet
> Ripe grace now ends in glory, so is he
> Sounding triumphs with the hierarchy.
>
> *Rev. Richard Russell.*

South Hill, Cornwall.

> Strange that this stone should tell
> Of saint turned Angel Michael :
> Stranger that so high a Hill
> Should sink so low a vault to fill :
> Strangest, when next we fleet
> If two and all we Hills should meet.
>
> 1663. *Michael Hill.*

Launceston, Cornwall.

The Husband's Valediction.

> Blest soul since thou art fled into the slumbers of the dead
> Why should mine eyes
> Let fall unfruitful tears, the offspring of despair and fears,
> To interrupt thy obsequies
> No, no, I won't lament to see thy day of trouble spent :
> But since thou art gone,
> Farewell ! sleep, take thy rest, upon a better husband's breast
> Until the resurrection.
>
> 1667. *Sarah Ruddle.*

St. Stephen Dunhered, Cornwall.

> Tis my request
> My bones may rest
> Within this chest
> Without molest.

> 1727.   *George Warmington.*

Tintagel, Cornwall.

On a man killed by lightning.

> The body that here buried lies
> By lightning's fell death's sacrifice
> To him Elijah's fate was given
> He rode on flames of fire to Heaven.
> Then mourn no more he's taken hence
> By the just hand of Providence.
> O God, the judgments of thy seat
> Are wondrous good and wondrous great
> Thy ways on all thy works appear
> As thunders loud as lightnings clear.

> 1702.   *Thomas Heminge.*

Wolverton, Somerset.

Here is a touching inscription on a little boy of eight who was run over by a waggon.

> The Lord was pleased his power to show
> In giving me a mortal throw,
> Which was from off a waggon's head
> Crushed with the wheels as it was said
> Let this my death a warning be
> The young or old I plainly see
> Must go when death doth for you call
> Appointed time there is for all.

> 1747.   *William West.*

Sherbourne Abbey, Dorset.

The following epitaph was written by Alexander Pope, the poet.

> Go, fair example of untainted youth,
> Of modest reason and pacific truth :
> Composed in sufferings, and in joy sedate,
> Good without noise, without pretention great.
> Go, just of word, in every thought sincere,
> Who knew no wish but what the world might hear :
> Of gentlest manners, unaffected mind,
> Lover of peace, a friend of human kind ;
> Go, live, for heaven's eternal year is thine,
> Go, and exalt thy mortal to divine.
> And thou, too close attendant on his doom,
> Blest maid, hast hastened to the silent tomb ;
> Steered the same course to the same quiet shore,
> Nor parted long, and now to part no more
> Go then, where only bliss sincere is known,
> Go, where to love and to enjoy are one !
> Yet take these tears, Mortality's relief,
> And, till we share your joys, forgive our grief ;
> These little rites, a stone and verse, receive
> 'Tis all a father, all a friend can give.
>
> *Robert and Mary Digby. Children of Lord Digby.*

Stourton Caundle, Dorset.

> The fates John Whittle to the clay
> And prison clothes have sent :
> His lease was out, he could not stay,
> For Death would have his rent.
> Cover'd with dust the farmer lies
> By Deborah confin'd ;
> When trumpet sounds, these doves will rise
> And leave their chains behind.
>
> 1721. *John Whittle and Deborah his wife.*

SALTFORD, SOMERSET.

Stop Reader and wonder ! see as strange as e'er was known,
My feet dropt off from my body, in the midst of the bone.
I had no surgeon for my help, but God Almighty's aid,
On whom I always will rely and never be afraid.
Tho' here beneath interred they lie, corruption for to see,
Yet shall they rise and reunite to all Eternity.

1723. Frances Flood.

WINCHESTER CATHEDRAL.

The following epitaph to Isaak Walton (Pixator) is
supposed to have been written by Bishop Ken.

> Alas ! he's gone before
> Gone to return no more
> Our panting breasts aspire
> After their aged Sire,
> Whose well-spent Life did last
> For ninety years, and past,
> But now he hath begun
> That which will ne'er be done,
> Crown'd with eternal bliss :
> We wish our souls with his.

1683.

EWERNE MINSTER, DORSET.

> Reader behold me ; I return to dust
> Yet at the resurrection of the just,
> My body to my soul shall be united,
> To love with Christ, in whom I have delighted.

1716. Mary Tilly.

EWERNE MINSTER, DORSET.

O thou most beloved sister and dearest friend,
let me thus bid thee a sorrowful, but as my
Soul hopes, not an everlasting farewell.

1758. Jane Wyatt.

St. Winnion, Cornwall.

When he had served his God, his Church, his Friend,
His Family, 'twas fit his life should end :
As then he had no more strength to bestow,
And God for him had no more work to do.
Even as a guest well fed with nature's stores,
Thankful and pleased, steps slowly out of doors,
So did he leave the world, went off the stage
Gently, not cloy'd, but satisfied with age.
More time he asked not, but obey'd the call
That then did him, at last shall summon all.

1713. *Edmund Stephens. Aged* 72.

Elton, Dorset.

The bodys here of two divines embrace,
Both which were once the Pastors of this place :
And if their corps each other seem to greet,
What will they do when soul and body meet ?

1669. *Robert Roch and John Antrem.*

Bath Abbey.

This epitaph on " Beau Nash " was written by Dr. Harington.

If social virtues make remembrance dear,
Or manners pure on decent rule depend :
To *His* remains consign one grateful tear.
Of youth the Guardian and of all the Friend.

Now sleeps dominion : here no Bounty flows,
Nor more avails this festive scene to grace,
Beneath that hand which no discernment shews
Untaught to honour, or distinguish place.

1761. *Richard Nash.*

WRAXALL, DORSET.

> Goodness in heaven gave a birth
> In her to goodness here on earth :
> And having time long with her blest
> Took her to heaven there to rest.
> Goodness on earth doth now in mourning go,
> Because she hath no pattern here below.

> 1672. *Elizabeth Lawrence.*

ASHBRIDGE, SOMERSET. On a Clockmaker.

> Bilbie, thy
> Movements kept in play
> For thirty years and more we say,
> Thy Balance or thy
> Mainspring's broke
> And all thy movements cease to work.

> 1767. *John Bilbie.*

MAKER, CORNWALL.

> My wife so dear I've left behind
> With an aching heart and a troubled mind
> In Heaven I hope your Soul to see
> So lead your life for to come to me
> There pain and grief cannot annoy
> Nor yet eclipse our loving joy.

> 1781. *Aaron Bankers.*

STALBRIDGE, DORSET.

> Here lies a good and patient wife
> Who in her lifetime hated strife :
> A generous friend in time of need,
> And one who loved the poor to feed ;
> A loving wife, a tender mother :
> Tis hard to find out such another.

> 1794. *Susannah Phillips.*

BATH ABBEY.

In memory of Rebecca Leyborne
Interred at the foot of this pillar
Born June the 4th 1698
Deceased February 18, 1756
A wife more than twenty-three years to Robert
Leyborne, D.D.

Who never saw her once ruffled with anger,
Or heard her utter even a peevish word :
Whether pained or injured, the same good woman
In whose mouth, as in whose character,
was no Contradiction ;
Resigned, gentle, courteous, affable :
Without passion, tho' not without sense,
She took offence as little as she gave it :
She never was, or made an enemy :
To servants mild ; to relations kind :
To the poor a friend, to the stranger hospitable ;
Always caring how to please her husband,
Yet was her attention to the one thing needful,
How few will be able to equal,
What all should endeavour to imitate.

1756. *Rebecca Leyborne.*

CALTISTOCKE, DORSET.

Smitten friends !

Are angels sent on errands full of love :
For us they languish and for us they die :
And shall they languish, shall they die in vain ?
Ungrateful shall we grieve their hovering shades
Which wait the reformation in our hearts ?
Shall we disdain their silent, soft address
Their posthumous advice, and pious prayers ?

1800. *Elizabeth Chudleigh.*

BRISTOL CATHEDRAL.

The following epitaph on Rev. Samuel Love, Minor Canon, is by Mrs. Hannah More.

> When worthless grandeur fills the embellish'd urn
> No poignant grief attends the sable bier :
> But when distinguished excellence we mourn,
> Deep is the sorrow, genuine the tear.
>
> Stranger, shouldst thou approach this awful shrine,
> The merits of the honour'd dead to seek :
> The Friend, the Son, the Christian, the Divine,
> Let those who knew him, those who lov'd him, speak.
>
> Oh ! let them in some pause of anguish say,
> What zeal inspir'd, what faith enlarged his breast,
> How soon the unfettered spirit winged its way
> From earth to heaven—from blessing to be blest.
>
> 1773.

WOODBRIDGE, DORSET.

> Great God ! is this our certain doom
> And are we still secure ?
> Still walking downward to our tomb,
> And yet prepare no more.
>
> 1796. *Benjamin Cooutes and Betty his wife.*

BISHOP'S CAUNDLE, DORSET.

> Sober, though liberal, and though prudent, just :
> Trusty, though cautious whom she ought to trust :
> She passed through life respected and admired,
> To that blest Kingdom she so much desired.
>
> 1798. *Susanna Wheffen.*

Tong, Salop.

This epitaph on Sir Thomas Stanley who died in 1600, is ascribed to Shakespeare.

> Ask who lies here, but do not weep :
> He is not dead, he doth but sleep !
> This stony register is for his bones,
> His fame is more perpetual than these stones,
> And his own goodness with himself being gone
> Shall live when earthly monument is none.
>
> Not monumental stone preserves our fame,
> Nor sky aspiring pyramids our name.
> The memory of him for whom this stands,
> Shall outlive marble and defacer's hands :
> When all, to time's consumption shall be given
> *Stanley*, for whom this stands, shall stand in Heaven.

Cartmel, Lancs.

> Here before lieth interred
> Ethelred Thornburgh's corpse in dust.
> In Life, at Death, still firmly fixed
> On God to rest her steadfast trust.
> Her father Justice Carns was
> Her mother Katharine his wife,
> Her husband William Thornburgh was
> Whilst here she led this mortal life.
> The third of March in year of Grace
> One thousand five hundred ninety six
> Her soul departed this earthly place
> Of age nigh forty years and six
> To whose sweet soul heavenly Dwelling
> Our Saviour grant everlasting.

> 1596.   *Ethelreda Thornburgh.*

GREAT WALTHAM, ESSEX.

> Who lists to see and know himself
> May look upon this glass,
> And weigh the beaten paths of death
> Which he shall one day pass.
>
> Which way Thomas Wyseman
> With patient mind hath gone,
> Whose body here as death hath charged
> Lieth covered with this stone.
>
> Thus dust to dust is brought again,
> The earth she hath her own :
> This shall the last of all men be,
> Before the trump is blown.
>
> 1600.   *Thomas Wyseman.*

ELINGHAM, NORFOLK.

This is one of the earliest of the many epitaphs with play
on the name More, or Moore.

> More had I once, More would I have,
>   More is not to be had :
> The first I lost the next is vain
>   The third is too too bad.
> If I had used with more regard,
>   The More that I did give,
> I might have made more use and fruit
>   Of More while he did live.
> But time will be recall'd no More,
>   More since are gone in brief.
> Too late repentance yields no More
>   Save only pain and grief.
> My comfort is that God hath More
>   Such Mores to send at will,
> In hope whereof I sigh no More
>   But rest upon him still.
>
> — *More, of Norwich.*   1600.

BABRAHAM, CAMBS.

> Here lies Horatio Palvicene
> Who robb'd the page to lend the Queen
> He was a thief.   A thief ! thou h'est :
> For why ? He robbed but Antichrist
> Him Death with besom swept from Babram
> Into the bosom of old Abram
> But then came Hercules with his Club,
> And struck him down to Beelzebub.

> > 1600.   *Horatio Palvicene.*

PETERBOROUGH CATHEDRAL.

> You see old Scarlett's picture stand on high,
> But at your feet there doth his body lie !
> His gravestone doth his age and death time show,
> His office by these tokens ye may know.
> Second to none for strength and sturdy limb,
> A Scar-babe mighty, voice and visage grim :
> He had interred two Queens within this place,
> And this town's householders in his life's space
> Twice over.   But at length his own turn came,
> What he for others did, for him the same
> Is done.   No doubt his soul doth live for aye
> In Heaven, though here his body's clad in clay.

> > 1594.   *R. Scarlett.   Aged* 98

HADLEY, MIDDLESEX.

> An ill year of a Goodyere us bereft
> Who gone to God, much lack of him here left :
> Full of good gifts, of body and of mind
> Wise, comely, learned, eloquent and kind.

> > 1604.   *Sir Henry Goodyere.*

St. John Maddermarket, Norwich.

> Under this cold marble sleeps
> He for whom even marble weeps
> His name lives here in good men's hearts
> Whilst Heaven enjoys the better parts.
> The race of fifty years and three
> His life ran out religiously
> Of gentle blood more worthy merit
> Whose breast enclosed an humble spirit.
> Oh ! death—thou hast the body won
> Of worthy Thomas Sothertone.
> His virtues 'bove thy power is raised
> And shall while time shall last be praised
> His one year's father Norwich chose him
> And wished that she might never lose him
> So dear a friend unto her state
> Is reft from her by cruel fate
> But 'twas decreed all that hath breath
> Must pass the womb to grave by death :
> So all must tread the path that he hath done
> And by death follow worthy Sothertone.

> 1608. *Thos. Sothertone.*

St. Gregory's, Norwich.

In remembrance of whose piety and singular virtues, the eternal love of her husband hath caused this Monument to be erected.

> In Heaven her soul, in me her love,
> Her body resteth here :
> Which is to God, was to the world,
> To me her husband, dear.

> 1598. *Mary Sandys.*

This is a sixteenth century epitaph at Little Bradley, Suffolk, to John Daye, the printer of Foxe's Book of Martyres. His widow subsequently married a man named Stone, which fact and her loneliness she ingenuously relates. Note the play on the name Daye.

Here lies the Daye that darkness could not blind
When popish fogs had overcast the sun
This Daye the cruel night did leave behind
To view and show what bloody Acts were done,
He set a Fox to write how martyrs run
By death to life.   Fox ventured pains and health ;
To give them light Daye spent in print his wealth
But God with gain returned his wealth again
And gave to him ; as he gave to the poor,
Two wives he had partakers of his pain
Alice was last increaser of his store,
Who mourning long for being left alone
Set up this tomb, herself turned to a *Stone.*

Plays on names in epitaphs were favourite diversions in the sixteenth century. Here is one from Barrow-on-Soar, Leicestershire, dated 1584, on one Theophilus Cave.

Here in this grave there lies one Cave :
We call a cave a grave.
If cave be grave, and grave be cave
  Then reader judge I crave
Whether both Cave be in this grave
  or grave lie here on Cave :
If grave in cave here would lie
Then grave, where is thy victory ?

Go reader and report
  Here lies a Cave
  Who conquers death
And buries his own grave.

H

A favourite epitaph, of which one of the oldest examples is on the grave of John Orgen, 1591, at St. Olave's, Hart Street, is the following :

> As I was so be ye : as I am you shall be
> What I gave, that I have
> What I spent, that I had
> Thus I count all my cost
> That I left, that I lost.

ELMSET, SUFFOLK.

Here lieth the body of Edward Sherland, of Grays Inn, Esqre, descended from the ancient family of Sherland in the Isle of Sheppey, in Kent ; who lived the whole of his life a single man, and died in this parish the 13th of May, 1609.

> Tombs have no use unless it be to show
> The due respect which friend to friend doth owe.
> Tis not a mausolean monument
> Or hireling epitaph that doth prevent
> The flux of fame : a painted sepulchre
> Is but a rotten trustless treasure,
> A fare gate to oblivion.
> But the whole life, whose every action,
> Like well-wrought stones and pyramids, erect
> A monument to honour and respect,
> As this man did, he needs none other hearse,
> Yet hath but due, having both tomb and verse.

HERNE, KENT.

> Here lies a piece of Christ, a star in dust,
> A view of gold, a china dish that must
> Be used in Heaven when God shall feed the just
> Approved by all, and loved so well,
> Tho' young, like fruit that's ripe, he fell.

1637. *John Knowles.*

WATERPERRY, OXON.

She that lies here within this gloomy grave
Enjoyed all virtues that a mind could have
Let this suffice thee then in brief to know
She once was such as thou mayst read below.
Lord Dormer's daughter, Sir John Curson's wife
To whom four sons and daughters two she bore
Beloved of all the lived yet chang'd this life
For such a life as never shall change more
A Magdalen by name, a Saint by Grace,
Died much bewailed and buried in this place,
Then happy she who such a life did lead
As she now lives anew though she is dead.

1610. *Magdalen Curson.*

TURVEY, BEDS.

Here lieth John Richards under this wall,
A faithful true servant to Turvey old Hall,
Page to the first Lord Mordaunt of fame,
Servant to Lewes, Lord Henry and John ;
Painful and careful and just to them all
Till death took his life
God have mercy of his soul. Amen.

1612. *John Rychards.*

ST. PETER'S, YOXFORD.

At the due sacrifice of the Paschal lamb,
April had eight days wept in showers, then came
Lean hungry death who never pity took,
And 'cause the feast was ended slew this *Cooke*
On Easter-Monday he lives then no day more,
But sunk to rise with Him that rose before
He's here entombed, a man of virtue's line
Outreached his years, yet they were seventy-nine
He left on earth ten children of eleven
To keep his name whilst himself went to Heaven.

1613. *Anthony Cooke.*

HIGH KIRK, GLASGOW.

> Stay passenger, and view this stone,
> For under it lies such an one,
> Who cured many while he lived,
> So gracious he no man grieved.
> Yea, when his physic's force oft failed
> His pleasant purpose then prevailed.
> For of his God he got the Grace
> To live in mirth and die in peace
> Heaven has his soul, his corpse this stone
> Sigh passenger, and then begone.

1612. Dr. Low.

ST. BENET—SHEREBOG.

> Here was a Bud, beginning for her May :
> Before her flower, Death took her hence away.
> But for what cause ? That friends might joy the more
> Where their hope is, she flourisheth now before.
>> She is not lost, but in those joys remain
>> Where friends may see and joy in her again.

1613. Anne Ferrar. Aged 21.

IVER, BUCKS.

> Here the earthly mansion of a heavenly mind,
> A worthy Matron's mortal part, is shrined.
> More might be said, if any tomb or stone
> Were large enough for her inscription.
> But words are bootless, more elegies hurled
> Upon her hearse were vain, for to the world
> Like a vain glorious gamester, 'twould but boast
> Not what it hath, but what it has lost :
> And making her life known, would cause my fear
> 'Twas greater than virtue's strength would bear.

1613. Lady Mary Salter.

Bolsover, Derby.

The epitaph is an address of Sir Charles Cavendish to his sons.

> Sons, seek me not among these polished stones,
> Those only hide part of my flesh and bones :
> Which they did here so neat or proudly dwell,
> Will all be dust and may not make me swell.
>
> Let such as have outlived all praise
> Trust in the tombs their careful friends do raise :
> I made my life my monument, and yours,
> To which there's no material that endures ;
> Nor yet inscription like it. Write one that
> And teach your nephews it to emulate :
> It will be matter loud enough to tell
> Not when I died, but how I lived. Farewell.
>
> 1617.

Shakespeare's epitaph at Stratford-on-Avon is one of the best known.

> Good friend, for Jesus sake forbear
> To dig the dust enclosed here
> Blest be the man that spares these stones
> And curst be he that moves my bones,

This inscription is on the gravestone—on the North Wall of the Chancel is a mural tablet with this inscription.

> Stay passenger, why goest thou by so fast,
> Read if thou canst, whom envious Death hath placed
> Within this monument, Shakespeare with whom
> Quick nature died : whose name doth deck the tomb,
> Far more then cost : Since all that he hath writ
> Leaves living art one page to serve his wit.
>
> 1616.

MICKLEHAM, GLOS.

The writer of this epitaph apparently had not a very great opinion of the residents of his county.

> Here lieth entombed John Bonner by name,
> Son of Bonner of Pebworth, from there he came.
> The 17th of October he ended his days
> Pray God that we living may follow his ways.

> *1618 by the year.*

> Scarce are such to be found in this Shere
> Made and set up by his loving friend
> *Evens* his kinsman, and so I do end.

> 1618.   *John Bonner.*

STOKENHAM, DEVON.

Here is an acrostic epitaph on a woman who was killed in an attack on the place during the Civil wars.

> Kind reader judge, here's underlaid
> A hopeful, young, and virtuous maid,
> Thrown from the top of earthly pleasure
> Headlong, by which she gained a measure
> Environed with heaven's power.
> Rounded with angels for that hour
> In which she fell : God took her home
> Not by just law, but martyrdom.
> Each groan she fetched upon her bed
> Roar'd out alone I'm murdered.
> And shall this blood, which here doth lie
> 'N vain for right and vengeance cry !
> Do men not think, tho' gone from hence,
> Avenge God can't his innocence ?
> Let bad men think, so learn ye good
> Love each that's here doth cry for blood.

> 1648.   *Katherine Randall.*

PENSHURST, KENT.

> Robert Kerwin now here doth lie,
> A man of proved honesty :
> Whose soul to Heaven hence did fly
> To enjoy Christ his felicity,
> The seventh of February—1615.

ARRETON, ISLE OF WIGHT.

Sixteen a maid and fifty years a wife
Make the sum total of my past life.
Long Thread, so finely spun, so fairly ended,
That few shall match this pattern, fewer mend it.
What friends, what children, what blest marriage,
Dead I forget : living I light esteemed
For thy dear love (O Christ) that has redeemed
My soul from Hell ; and shortly shall upraise
This mortal Dust, in Heaven to sing thy praise.

> 1619. *Elizabeth Leigh.*

> This Mary-gold lo here doth show
> Marie worth gold lies here below
> Cut down by death the fair'st gilt flower
> Flourish and fade doth in an hour
> The Marigold in sunshine spread
> (When cloudy) closed doth bow the head.
> This orient plant retains the guise
> With splendent Sol to set and rise
> Even so this virgin Marie rose
> In Life soon nipt in death fresh grows
> With Christ her light she set in pain
> By Christ her Lord shall rise again
> When she shall shine more brightly far
> Than any twinkling radiant star
> For be assured that by death's dart
> Mary enjoys the better part.

CURIOUS EPITAPHS

CURIOUS EPITAPHS

No collection of epitaphs would be complete without special reference to the many quaint, curious, humorous and sometimes ludicrous epitaphs often found on tombstones. Many of those already given under the heading of "Ancient Epitaphs" would justify inclusion in this category, but the following may perhaps have a special claim to insertion under this heading. Most of them are authenticated, but a few have been added which if not actually inscribed upon tombstones are *ben trovat*.

IVER CHURCH.

> Two happy days assigned me to men,
> Of wedlock and of death! Oh, happy then!
> 'Mongst women was she that is here interred,
> Who liv'd out two, and dying had the third.
>
> 1634. *Alice Cutt, aged* 55.

SOUTHREY.

> Here rests that just and pious Jane,
> That ever hated all that's vayne;
> Her zeal for God, made her desire
> T'have died a martyr in the fire;
> Or into thousand pieces small,
> Been cutt to honour God with all,
> Her life right vertuous, modest, sober;
> Ended the 7th day of October, 1638.
> Her purest soul 'till the body rise,
> Enjoys heaven's peace in paradise.
> Her virtues hid from common sight,
> Enforced her husband these to write.
>
> 1638. *Jane Tyrrell.*

Wisbech.

Nicholas Sanford
He was

A patterne for townesmen, whom we may enrole
For at his own charge this towne hee freed of tole.

Sheepsdale.

Son of Thunder, Son of the Dove,
Full of hot zeal, full of trewe love.
In preaching Truth, in living right,
A burning Lamp, a shining Light.

1640. *Rev. John Rudd, aged* 72.

Icklesham.

Here lies George Theobald, a lover of bells,
And of this house, as that epitaph tells,
He gave a bell freely to grace the new steeple,
Bring out his prayse therefore ye good people.   1641.

St. James', Clerkenwell.

Thos. Wayte, of Keythorp, Esq.
Receiver for His Majesty in the Counties of
Warwick and Leicester.

1642.

Hither no Tears but Garlands bring,
  To crown this good Receiver's dust ;
Who gave account to God and King,
  And lives rewarded with the just.
So to his Faith and Office both gave rest
  The King his quittance, God *quietus est.*

Bushey.

Here's two in one, and yet not two but one,
Two sons, one tomb ; two heirs one name alone.

1643. *Robt. Blakewell.*

ACTON CHURCH.

Here lyes the body—— Hould ! someone replies,
'Tis not her body, 'tis this marble lyes ;
For her fayre clay, ere death could reach her bed,
Sly sickness (to cheat him) thence ravished,
And in its roome conveyed a skelleton,
Which scarce her looking glasse or friends could owne ;
A skelleton so bare, that as she lay,
She seemed a soule abstracted from its clay
Thus lighten'd, she could act and never faint,
But moved more like an angell than a saint ;
Whilst, through those weatherbeaten walls of skin,
Each looker-on might see what dwelt within :
Sound judgment, joyn'd to active piety,
But, sweetness, patience and humility.
A virgin too ! save that, just such another,
In all perfections as her neighbour mother.

1645. *Elizabeth Wilbraham.*

OLD GREY FRIARS, EDINBURGH.

Stay, Passenger, and shed a tear,
For good James Murray lieth here ;
He was of Philip Haugh descended,
And for his merchandize commended.
He was a man of a good life,
Marry'd Bethia Mauld to his wife :
He may thank God that e'er he got her,
She bore him three sons and a daughter.
The first he was a Man of Might,
For which the King made him a Knight.
The second was both wise and wily,
For which the Town made him a Bailly :
The third a Factor of Renown,
Both in Camphire and in this Town.
His daughter was both grave and wise
And married was to James Elies.

1649. *James Murray, aged* 78.

Yeovil, Somerset.

John Webb,
Son of Mary and John Webb, Clothiers,
Who died of the measles, May 3rd, 1646,
Aged 3 years.

How still he lies !
And clos'd his eyes,
That shone as bright as day !
The cruel measles
Like clothiers' teasles
Have scratched his life away.

Cochineal red
His lips have fled,
Which now are blue and black.
Dear pretty wretch
How thy limbs stretch,
Like cloth upon the rack.

Repress thy sighs
The husband cries,
My dear, and not repine,
For ten to one,
When God's work's done
He'll come off superfine.

St. Edmund's, Sarum. 1662.

Richard Phelps,
Alderman and Mayor.

And is he dead ! And shan't the City weep ?
That it no longer such a Saint could keep.
Surely when Death shall thus lay Hold upon
The Pillars of the House, the Building's gone.
Well may we fear and dread what God is doing
That Flames are kindling while our Lots are going.
The righteous is taken away
From the evil to come.

GLOUCESTER CATHEDRAL.

> Receiver of this College Rents, he paid
> His Debt to Nature, and beneath he's laid
> To rest, until his summons to remove,
> At the last Audit, to the Choir above.
>
> 1650. *Samuel Bridger.*

WITCHINGHAM.

> Death here advantage hath of life I spye
> One husband with two wives at once may lye.
>
> 1650. *Thos. Alleyn and his two wives.*

EVESHAM.

> Stay reader, drop upon this stone
> One pitying tear, and then be gone.
> A handsome pyle of flesh and blood
> Is here sunk down to its first mud,
> Which thus in Western rubbish lyes,
> Until ye Eastern Starr shall rise.
>
> 1652. *John Green, aged 27.*

PETERBOROUGH CATHEDRAL.

> Heare lyeth a midwife brought to bed,
> Deliveresse Delivered ;
> Her body being Churched here
> Her soule gives thanks in yonder sphere.
>
> 1653. *Jane Parker.*

NORTH TUDENHAM.

> Here lyes the corps of Frances Neve interred,
> This Virgin's Soul to Heaven is transferred.
> April laments her death, tho' born in May
> When Flora her perfections doth display.
>
> 1656. *Frances Neve.*

KINGSTON-UPON-THAMES.

> Ashes on ashes lie, on Ashes tread
> Ashes engrav'd these words, which Ashes read,
> Then what poor thing is Man, when every gust
> Can blow his Ashes to their Kindred Dust ?
> More was intended, but a wind did rise,
> And filled with Ashes both my mouth and eyes.
>
> 1655.   *Thos. Haward, aged* 76.

TAWSTOCK.

> Under this Marble lies a Treasure
> Which Earth hath lost and Heaven gain'd,
> Wherein we Mortals took just Pleasure
> While his blest soul on earth remain'd.
>   A lawyer who desir'd to see
>   His Clients Right more than his Fee.
>
> 1660.   *Alexander Rolle, aged* 48.

IN WESTMINSTER ABBEY.

In memory of Mr. Thos. Smith, of Elmley Lovet, in the County of Worcester, and Bachelor of Arts, late of Christ's Church, Oxford, who through the Spotted Veil of the Small Pox, render'd a pure and unspotted soul to God, expecting but never fearing Death which ended his days, March 10th A.D. 166¾, aged 27.

> The virtues which in his short Life were shown
> Have equalled been by few, surpassed by none.

EAST BRADENHAM.   1667.

> Here virtuous, pious Sarah Townsend lies
> Whose soul enamell'd thus, to Heaven flies.

NORWICH. 1669.

Here lays Captain Nicholas Salter, whose
Choice Endowments both in Grace and Art,
Deserve the ablest Hand to express but Part,
As to Religion constant and sincere,
Faithful and fervent, fighting while h'was here,
The Fight of Faith, o'ercome, and is sett downe,
His Course he finish'd, and enjoys a Crowne ;
And for his Art and Ingenuity,
By his exquisite Skill in Turning, Hee
Made so conspicuous, that who it beheld,
Was at his Art with Admiration filled,
But cease, no more, only a Sword, a Tear,
To lett the Reader know, choice Dust lies here.

1670. On GEORGE FANE.

Here lies a child, whose death has set us right,
In the old story of our guardian knight,
For who dare say the champion smells o' the forge,
Since we are all assur'd there's a St. George
Who ne'er was vanquish'd, nor o'ercome ;
For he is still alive by a synecdoche.*

* A synecdoche is a figure of speech by which a part is put for
the whole, and the contrary.

GLASTONBURY.

Whom neither Sword nor Gunn in War
Could slay, in Peace a cough did marr,
'Gainst Rebels He and Lust and Sin
Fought the good Fight, died Life to win.

1670. *Captain John Dyer.*

RICHMOND, YORKS.

Here lies the body of William Wix
One thousand, seven hundred and sixty-six.

I

LEDBURY, HEREFORD. 1674.

Stay reader,
Here lyes the body of James Bailey, late of Ledbury,
Corvisor, who departed this life 13 Dec. 1674.
Aged 100 years and 8 months. He was the
youngest brother of Humphrey Bailey of Ocul
Pychard, and of Samuel Bailey, late of Hereford.
These three brothers lived the age of 300 years.
What one wanted the
Other made up. *Mors rapit omnia.*

TEDSTON-DE-LA-MERE.

Heav'n took her soule ; the earth her corpse did seise,
Yet not in fee ; she only holds by lease,
With this proviso—when the Judge shall call,
Earth shall give up her share, and Heav'n take all.

1678. *Frances Bateman.*

NEWPORT, MON.

Stay, Gentle Reader, stay, drop down one tear
Though heart of flint and Eye of Pumice were,
Good, just, discreet, strong, debonaire and wise,
Man at his zenith midst death's trophies lies,
And bids the bravest at the best beware,
What ere thou art he was, thyself prepare.

1678. *William Morgan, aged* 48.

ST. DUNSTAN'S IN THE WEST.

A Master of Defence
His thrusts like Lightning flew, more Skilful Death
Parr'ed 'em all, and beat him out of Breath.

1679. *Alexander Layton.*

NORWICH CATHEDRAL.

Here lies the body of honest Tom Page
Who died in the 33rd year of his age.

WREXHAM.

Here lies John Shore
I say no more
Who was alive
In sixty five.

STEPNEY. 1683.

Whoever treadeth on this stone,
I pray you tread most neatly :
For underneath the same doth lie
Your honest friend Will Wheatly.

Here lies John Oxenham, a goodly young man, in whose chamber, as he was struggling with the pangs of death, a bird with a White Breast was seen fluttering about his bed, and so vanished.

Here also lies Mary Oxenham, sister of the above John, who died the next day, and the same apparition was in the room.

Here lies hard by, James Oxenham, the son of the said John, who died a child in his cradle, a little after, and such a bird was seen fluttering about his head a little before he expired, which vanished afterwards.

Here lies Elizabeth Oxenham, the mother of the said John, who died 16 years since, when such a bird, with a White Breast, was seen about her bed before her death.

To all these were divers witnesses, both Squires and Ladies, whose names were graven on the stone (seen by Howell at a stone-cutters in Fleet Street, and recorded in his letters) which was to be sent to a town hard by Exeter, where this happened.

St. Margaret's at Lynn. 1684.

William Scrivener,
Cook to the Corporation.

Alas! alas! Will Scrivener's dead, who by his art
Could make Death's Skeleton edible in each part.
Mourn, squeamish stomachs, and ye curious palates,
You've lost your dainty dishes and your salades :
Mourn for yourselves, but not for him i' th' least,
He's gone to taste of a more Heavenly feast.

Norwich. 1679.

Sarah Yorke this life did resigne
One May the 13th '79.

The following was written by Capt. Morris on Edward
Heardson, thirty years cook to the Beef-steak Society.

His last *steak* done ; his fire rak'd out and dead,
Dish'd for the worms himself, lies honest Ned.
We, then, whose breasts bore all his fleshly toils,
Took all his *bastings* and shared all his *broils* :
Now, in our turn, a mouthful carve and trim,
And dress at Phœbus fire, one scrap for him.
His heart which well might grace the noblest grave,
Was grateful, patient, modest, just and brave ;
And ne'er did earth's wide man a morsel gain
Of kindlier juices or more tender grain ;
His tongue, where duteous friendship humbly dwell,
Charm'd all who heard the faithful zeal he felt ;
Still to whatever end his *chops* he moved,
'Twas all *well-seasoned, relish'd* and approved ;
This room his heav'n—when threatening Fate drew nigh
The closing shade that dimm'd his lingering eye,
His last fond hopes, betray'd by many a tear,
Were—That his life's last spark might glimmer here ;
And the last words that choak'd his parting sigh—
" Oh! at your feet, dear masters, let me die! "

BARNSTAPLE.

> Blest was the prophet in his Heavenly shade
> But oh ! how soon did his umbrella fade.
> Like our frail bodies which being born of clay
> Spring in a night and wither in a day.
>
> 1684.　*John Boyse, aged* 5.

On a Brass in Aughton Church, near Ormskirk.

> Jesus Salvator
> My ancestors have been interred here above 380 years,
> This to me by ancient evidence appears ;
> Which that all may know and none doe offer wrong,
> It is ten feet and one inch broad, and foure yards and
> a half long.　　　　　AMEN.

RICHARD MOSSOCK. 1686.

> " God save the King to the greate glory of God."

At Kenning-hill Churchyard in Norfolk, one of the name of Robert Burton is stated to have died on the 29th of June, between 6 and 7 o'clock in the evening. In the anxiety to record the precise hour of his death the year is omitted. It was, however, in 1711.

HAMPTON RIDWARE, STAFFS.

Underneath lies the body of Thomas Allestree, M.A., late rector of this parish, and prebendary of Lichfield, who was a minister of the Church of England 54 years. He composed 500 sermons, and preached above 5,000 times. He died the 30th day of June 1715 in the 78th year of his age.

ST. CUTHBERT, KILDALE, YORKS.

Joseph Dunn.

Here lyeth the body of Joseph Dunn, who dyed ye 10th day of March, 1716, aged 82 years. He left to ye poor of Kildale xxs, of Commondale xxs, of Danby xxs., of Westerdale xs. to be paid upon his gravestone by equal portions, on ye 1st day of May, and ye 11th of November for ever.

ST. PAUL'S, BEDFORD.

Patience, wife of Shadrach Johnson,
The mother of 24 children and died in childbed
June 6, 1717, aged 38 years.

Shadrach ! Shadrach !
The Lord granted unto thee
Patience
Who laboured long and patiently
In her vocation ;
But her *patience* being exhausted
She departed in the midst of her labour
obiit 38.
May she rest from her labour.

Gentle Reader, Gentle Reader,
Look on the spot where I do lie
I was always a very good feeder
But now the worms do feed on I.

NORWICH.

Let Charity this man commend
To diligent apprentices, whose end
Brought money to their city : stock to lend.

1690. *Roger Crewe, aged* 51.

New Windsor.

> Reader, this monument does here declare,
> That Richard Topham was John Topham's heir,
> And that this secret might to all be known
> Richard hath writ it on John Topham's stone.
> The language view, and own the pious deed,
> Since Richard writes, what John could never read.
>
> 1692. John Topham.

Limerick Cathedral.

> Memento Mory.
> Here lieth little Samuel Barinton, that great Under
> Taker,
> Of Famous City's Clock and Chime Maker;
> He made his one Time goe Early and Latter,
> But now he is returned to God his Creator.
>
> The 19 of November Then he Seest,
> And for his memory this here is pleast
> By his Son Ben, 1693.

Sarnsfield, 1694.

> On John Abel, Architect.
>
> This craggy stone a covering is for an architector's bed
> That lofty buildings raised high, yet now lies low
> his head.
> His line and rule, so death concludes, are locked up
> in stone,
> Build they that list or they that wist for he can build
> no more.
> His house of clay could hold no longer,
> May heaven's joy build him a stronger.

DUNSTER, NORFOLK.

> Here lies a noble pair, who were in name,
> In Heart, in Mind, and Sentimentt the same,
> The Arithmetick Rule then can't be true,
> For *One* and *One*, did never here make *Two*.
>
> > 1709-1720. *Israel and Sarah Long.*

MARY TAVY, DEVON.

> Here Buried were some years before
> His Two Wives and Five Children more,
> One Thomas nam'd whose fate was such
> To lose his life by wrestling much
> Which may a warning be to all
> How they into such Pastimes fall.
> Elizabeth and William and
> Hannah, and yet pray understand
> A second nam'd Elizabeth
> All these were taken off by Death
> For which prepare you Readers all
> We must away when God doth call.
>
> > 1721. *Thomas Hawkins, aged* 28.

CHURCH CRETON, SALOP.

> On a Thursday she was born,
> On a Thursday made a bride,
> On a Thursday put to bed,
> On a Thursday broke her leg, and
> On a Thursday died.

SOUTH BREWHAM.

To the ever living memory of the Rev. Edward Bennet, minister of the Gospel, who by a sudden-surprize fell asleep in Christ, the 8th day of November, 1673. Aged 50. And Mary, his wife, who also by a sudden-surprize fell asleep in Christ, Feb. 26th, 1694. Aged 79.

St. Dunstan's, Stepney. 1687.

> Here Thomas Saffin lies interred : Ah ! why ?
> Born in New England did in London die ?
> Was the third son of eight ; begot upon
> His mother Martha, by his Father John ;
> Much favor'd by his Prince he got to be
> But nipt by Death at th' age of twenty-three ;
> Fatal to him was that, sad Small Pox name
> By which his Mother and two Brethren came
> Also to breathe their last ; nine years before ;
> And now have left their father to deplore
> The loss of all his children with that wife
> Who was the joy and comfort of his life.

Wolverhampton Church. 1690.

> Here lie the bones
> of Joseph Jones,
> Who eat whilst he was able ;
> But once o'er fed
> He dropt down dead,
> And fell beneath the table.
> When from the tomb,
> To meet his doom,
> He rises amidst sinners :
> Since he must dwell
> In heav'n or hell
> Take him—which gives best dinners.

Edmonton Churchyard. 1695.

On William Newberry, a hostler, who lost his life from the improper administration of medicine by an ignorant fellow servant.

> Here lies Newberry Will
> His life was finished with a Cochiæ Pill.

KENDAL.

Frances Strickland.

She was born ⎱
    Married ⎰ 24 June ⎰ 1690.
    Buried ⎰   ⎰ 1708.
                    1725.

Emblem of temporal good, the day that gave
Her birth and marriage, saw her in her grave ;
Wing'd with its native love her soul took flight
To boundless regions of eternal light.

Great eaters have been frequently celebrated in epitaphs,
of which the following are specimens.

On a great Epicure.

At this rude stone, ye sons of Bacchus pause ;
Here lies a martyr to the *good old cause* ;
A doctor fam'd for most voracious parts,
Profoundly versed in culinary arts ;
Skilled in the merits of renowned sirloin,
Nor less *de vino* proved a sound divine.
Long shall the generous juice embalm his clay,
Nor vulgar worms upon this carcass prey.
Full many a sparkling stream his lips have quaffed,
But relished not this last and bitter draughte ;
So strong the potion proved, or weak his head
Here lies our doctor—down among the dead.
                         T. Maurice.

On a Glutton.

At length, my friends, the feast of life is o'er,
I've eat sufficient, and I'll drink no more ;
My night is come, I've spent a jovial day,
'Tis time to part, but oh !—what is to pay ?

Randolph Peter
Of Oriel the eater.
Whoe'er you are, tread softly, I entreat you,
For if he chance to wake, be sure he'll eat you.

Here lies Johnny Cole,
Who died, on my soul,
After eating a plentiful dinner ;
While chewing his crust,
He was turned into dust,
With his crimes undigested—poor sinner.

St. Mary's, York. 1696. Accidentally drowned.

Nigh to the River Ouse, in York's fair city,
Unto this pretty maid, death shew'd no pity ;
As soon as she'd her pail with water filled,
Came sudden Death and life like water spilled.

Staplehurst.

Here lies a piece of Heaven (t'others above)
Which shortly goes up to the world of love
The brightest sweetest angels must convey
This spotless virgin on the starry way,
That glittering quire sings but a lisping song
'Till she appears amidst the shining throng.

1703. *Mary, daughter of W. Mayo.*

Selby, Yorks. 1706.

Here lies the body of poor Frank Row,
Parish Clerk, and grave stone cutter.
And this is writ to let you know,
What Frank for others us'd to do,
Is now for Frank done by another.

LAUDER.

Alexander Thompson.

Here lyes interred an honest man,
Who did this churchyard first lie in ;
This monument shall make it known
That he was the first laid in this ground.
Of mason and of masonerie
He cutted stones right curiously.
To heaven we hope that he is gone,
Where Christ is the Chief Corner Stone.

WILTON.

At twenty years of age I little thought,
That hither to this place I should been brought,
Therefore as in the Lord I put my trust,
I hope I shall be blessed among the Just.

1725.   *Elizabeth Bell.*

RUDGWICK.

Here lies the body of Cranley, Doctor Edward Haynes,
Who for to maintain his family spar'd not for pains :
　　To ride and to run, to give relief
　　To those that were in pain, in grief.
He, the 30th of April, entered Death's straight gate,
In the year of our Lord, one thousand seven hundred
　　and eight.
He left behind him when he left this life
Two likely sons and a loving wife ;
　　And, about 36 weeks after
His wife and relict was brought to bed with a daughter ;
　　Which three we desire may live,
　　Not to beg, but to give.
His eldest son Edward, about six years and ten months' old,
His youngest son, John, three, both dapper and bold.
Like to most mortals, to his business he was a slave,
Catched the small-pox and died, and lies here in his grave.

HEGDON.

Here lyeth the body of
William Strutton of Padrington
Buried the 18th of May, 1734.
Aged 97.
Who had, by his first wife, twenty-eight children
And by second seventeen
Own father to forty-five
Grand-father to eighty-six
Great grandfather to ninety-seven
And great great grandfather to twenty-three
In all, two hundred and fifty-one.

In Laurence Lideard Churchyard one similar.

The man that rests in this grave has had 8 wives, by
whom he had 45 children, and 20 grandchildren.
He was born rich, lived and died poor, aged 94 years.
July 30, 1774.
Born at Bewdley in Worcestershire in 1650.

1705.   On Edward Jones, Gazette Printer of the Savoy.

Here lies a Printer, famous in his time !
Whose life by lingering sickness did decline ;
He lived in credit, and in peace he died,
And often had the chance of Fortune tried ;
Whose smiles by various methods did promote
Him to the favour of the Senate's vote ;
And so became by national consent,
The only Printer for the Parliament ;
Thus by degrees, so prosp'rous was his fate
He left his heirs a very good estate.

EDWALLON, NOTTS.

She drank good ale, good punch and wine
And lived to the age of 99.

1741.   *Rebecca Freeland.*

CHISWICK.

Here lyes ye clay
which the other day
inclos'd Sam Sevill's soul,
but now is free and unconfined,
she fled and left her clay behind
Intombed within this mole
May ye 21, 1728
in the 30 year of his age.

WOLSTANTON.

Ann Jennings.
Some have children—some have none
Here lies the mother of twenty-one.

EYRIE, ABERDEENSHIRE.

Erected to the memory of Alexander Gray, some time farmer in Mill of Burns, who died in the 96th year of his age, having had 32 legitimate children by two wives.

ST. PETER'S EAST, OXFORD.

Here
lieth the body of
Thomas Hearne, M.A.,
who studied and preserved
antiquities. He died June 10th,
1735, aged 57 years.
Deut. xxxii, 7.
Remember the days of old, consider the years of many generations : ask thy father, and he will shew thee, thy elders, and they will tell thee.

ST. ANDREW'S, PLYMOUTH.

Here lies the body of James Vernon, Esq., only *surviving* son of Admiral Vernon ; died 23rd July, 1723.

St. Katherine's.

> March, with his winds, has struck a cedar tall,
> And weeping April mourn'd the cedar's fall;
> May intends no flowers to bring
> Because he has lost the flower of the spring.

> 1740. *Susannah Butts, aged* 79.

Kir-Keel.

Here lie the remains of Thomas Nicols who died in Philadelphia, March, 1753. Had he *lived* he would have been buried here.

> Under this sod lies John Round
> Who was lost in the sea and never was found.

Arlesford.

> No supervisor's check he fears
> Now no Commissioners obey
> He's free from cares, intreaties, tears
> And all the Heavenly Orb surveys.

> 1750. *Benjamin Browne, an Excise Officer.*

Ballast Hills, Newcastle.

> When I enjoyed this mortal life,
> This stone I ordered from Scotland's Fife,
> To ornament the burial place
> Of me, and all my human race.
> Here lies James, of tender affection,
> Here lies Isabel, of sweet complexion,
> Here lies Katherine, a pleasant child,
> Here lies Mary, of all most mild,
> Here lies Alexander, a babe most sweet,
> Here lies Janet, as the Lord saw meet.
> J. Steel, 1757.
> Here lies avarice (? averse) to strife
> A loving and a faithful wife.

Two on talkative old maids.

> Beneath this silent stone is laid
> A noisy, antiquated maid,
> Who from her cradle talked till death,
> And never before was out of breath.

> Here lies, returned to clay
> Miss Arabella Young,
> Who on the first of May
> Began to hold her tongue.

MONKNEWTON, NEAR DROGHEDA.

> Erected by Patrick Kelly,
> of the town of Drogheda, Mariner,
> in memory of his Posterity.
> Also the above Patrick Kelly
> who departed this life the 12th August, 1844.
> Aged 60 years.
> Requiescat in Pace.

Another eccentric epitaph from Oxfordshire.

> Here lies the body of John Eldred,
> At least he will be here when he is dead ;
> But now at this time he is alive
> The 14th of August, sixty-five.

BLAGDON.

> With Sappho's taste, with Arria's tender heart,
> Lucretia's honour, and Cecilia's art ;
> That such a woman died surprize can't give ;
> 'Tis only strange that such an one could live.

> 1768. *Ann Langhorne, aged 32.*

DARLINGTON.

> 1765. Richard Preston, Sexton.
> (Translated from the Latin.)

> Under this marble are deposed
> Poor Preston's sad remains.
> Alas! too true for light-robed jest
> To sing in playful strains.
> Ye dread possessors of the grave,
> Who feed on other's woe,
> Abstrain from Richard's small remains
> And grateful pity shew.
> For many a weighty corpse he gave
> To you with liberal hand ;
> Then sure his little body may
> Some small respect command.

BERMONDSEY. 1770.

Will Wylde, needlemaker to Queen Charlotte.

> Man wants but little, nor that little long ;
> How soon must he resign his very dust,
> Which frugal nature lent him but for one hour.

MAIDSTONE.

> Here lies a keeper bred and born
> To turn his back he thought it scorn
> He was a man that had good skill
> Many a brave buck and doe to kill
> But that bold archer Death, who conquers all,
> Shot him to the heart and caused him here to fall.
> In youth or age all flesh must die
> And turn to dust as well as I.

> 1773. *Thomas Bradshaw, aged* 82.

K

Marston.

> I would have my neighbours be all kind and mild,
> Quiet and civil to my dear wife and child.

1768. Robert Loden.

In Horsley-Down Church, Cumberland, is to be found this extraordinary epitaph.

Here lie the bodies
of Thomas Bond and Mary his wife.
She was temperate, chaste and charitable
But
She was proud, peevish and passionate.
She was an affectionate wife and a tender mother
But
her husband and child, whom she loved,
Seldom saw her countenance without a disgusting frown,
Whilst she received visitors, whom she despised,
With an endearing smile.
Her behaviour was discreet towards strangers ;
But
Independent in her family.
Abroad, her conduct was influenced by good breeding ;
But
At home, by ill temper.
She was a professed enemy to flattery,
and was seldom known to praise or commend ;
But
The talents in which she principally excelled
Were difference of opinion, and discovering
flaws and imperfections.
She was an admirable economist,
And, without prodigality,
Dispensed plenty to every person in her family
But
Would sacrifice their eyes to a farthing candle.
She sometimes made her husband happy
With her good qualities ;

But
Much more frequently miserable—with
her many failings.
Insomuch that in 30 years cohabitation he
often lamented
That maugre of all her virtues,
He had not, in the whole, enjoyed two years
of matrimonial comfort.
At length
Finding that she had lost the affections of her husband,
As well as the regard of her neighbours,
Family disputes having been divulged by servants,
She died of vexation, July 20, 1768,
Aged 48 years.
Her worn-out husband survived her
four months and two days
And departed this life, November 28, 1768
in the 54th year of his age.
William Bond, brother to the deceased, erected
this stone, as a *weekly monitor* to the
Surviving wives of this parish,
That they may avoid the infamy
Of having their memories handed to posterity
With a Patch-work Character.

FOLKESTONE.

We far from home did Come
Each other for to join,
In peace with all men here we Liv'd
And did in Love Combine,
But oh remark the Strange
Yet Heaven's wise decree,
I'm lodged within the silent grave,
He's rouling in the sea.

1777. *Martha, wife of John Wells.*

On Catherine Hall, celebrated as a tambour worker and an excellent player at whist.

> Ere my *work's* done, my *thread* is cut ;
> My hands are cold, my eyesight fails,
> Stretch'd in my *frame*, I'm compass'd now,
> With worms instead of lovely *snails* !*
> The *game* of life is finished too,
> Another now has ta'en my chair ;
> Grieved there's no *shuffling* after death,
> I'm gone, alas, the Lord knows where !
> Reader, attend, if you in *works* excel,
> In bliss eternal you'll hereafter dwell ;
> And if you *play your cards* with caution here,
> Secure to win, the *trump* you need not fear.

> * *Chenilles*, the silk twist used in tambour work.

At Birmingham, in his garden, in a tomb prepared by himself is the following inscription on

John Baskerville
Died in 1775.   Aged 69.

Stranger,
beneath this cone, in *unconsecrated* ground,
a friend to the liberties of mankind directed
his body to be inurn'd.
May the example contribute to emancipate
thy mind from the idle fears of superstition
and the wicked arts of Priesthood.

UPPER DENTON.

> What I was once some may relate,
> What I am now is each one's fate ;
> What I shall be none can explain,
> Till he that called, call again.

1777.   *Margaret Teasdale.*

KENSINGTON.

> Farewell, vain world ! I've had enough of thee ;
> I value not what thou canst say of me ;
> Thy smiles I value not, nor frowns don't fear ;
> All's one to me, my head is quiet here.
> What faults you've see in me, take care to shun,
> Go home, and see there's something to be done.

1776. *Thomas Wright.*

ST. JOHN'S, STAMFORD.

> Tho' hot my name, yet mild my nature,
> I bore good will to every creature ;
> I brewed good ale and sold it too,
> And unto each I gave his due.

1783. *William Pepper.*

KING STANLEY, GLOS.

> 'Twas as she tript from Cask to Cask,
> In at a bung-hole quickly fell,
> Suffocation was her task,
> She had no time to say farewell.

1804. *Ann Collins.*

HOMERSFIELD, SUFFOLK.

> " Myself."

> As I walked by myself I talked to myself,
>   And thus myself said to me,
> Look to thyself and take care of thyself
>   For nobody cares for thee.
> So I turn'd to myself, and I answered myself
>   In the self-same reverie
> Look to myself or look not to myself
>   The self-same thing will it be.

1810. *Robert Crytoft, aged* 90.

NEWTOWN, GRAVESEND.

> To the memory of Mr. Alderman Wynn,
> An honest Man and an excellent Bowler.

Full forty years was the Alderman seen
The delight of each bowler and king of this green ;
As long be remembered his art and his name
Whose hand was unerring, unrivalled his game.
His bias was good and he always was found
To the right way and to enough ground.
The Jack to the uttermost verge he would send
For the Alderman lov'd a full length at each end.
Now mourn every eye that has seen him display
The arts of the game and the wiles of his play
For the great bowler Death, at one critical cast
Has ended his length and close rubb'd him at last.

ISLINGTON.

She had no fault save what travellers give the moon :
Her light was lovely, but she died too soon.

> 1808. *Elizabeth Emma Thomas, aged* 27.

John Webster. Died 1809, aged 8.
(Killed by a cart-wheel going over his head.)

Ye little children that survey,
  The emblemed wheel that crush'd me down,
Be cautious, as you careless play,
  For shafts of death fly thick around.
Still rapid drives the car of time,
  Whose wheels one day shall crush you all ;
The cold, low bed that now is mine,
  Will soon be that of great and small.

STOKE NEWINGTON.

(An epitaph containing some practical advice.)

This tomb was erected by William Picket, of
the City of London, goldsmith, on the melancholy
death of his daughter Elizabeth.

A testimony of respect
from greatly afflicted parents.
In memory of Elizabeth Picket, spinster,
who died December 11, 1781.
Aged 23 years.
this much lamented
young person expired in consequence
of her clothes taking fire
the preceding evening.

Reader, if ever you should witness such an affecting
scene ; recollect that the only method to extinguish
the flame is to stifle it by an immediate covering.

So unaffected, so composed a maid,
So firm, yet soft ; so stout yet so refined ;
Heav'n as pure gold, by flaming tortures try'd.
The angel bore them, but the mortal dyed.
Not a sparrow falls
On the ground without
Our Heavenly Father.

JOVINGTON, SUSSEX. 1808.

Two children, aged 13 and 7.

Samuel and John Purland.

Parents dear, weep not for we
Though we were drowned in the sea
'Twas God that did ordain it so ;
And when he calls we all must go.

St. Andrew's, Newcastle.

Mary, wife of Robert M'Cutchin,
Sergeant in the Grenadier Guards, died May 11, 1781
in the 27th year of her age.

In all our marriage vows, she did fulfill
And fondly sought her husband, thro' the dead on
    Bunker's Hill.
At many actions more, and at the Brandy-Wine,
She lov'd her husband so, she would not stay behind.
Till now by cruel Death's dread dart,
She is left behind, and forc'd to part
Till the last trump, when Gabriel sounds amain
She'll rise, embrace and join again.

Lawrence Pountney. 1784.

Passenger
spare to obliterate the name of
Charles Rogers,
whose body is here deposited,
unless you are convinced that he hath
injured you by word or deed.

Henry Hudson,
late Hat-maker, Fore Street,
who died June, 1787, while eating his Breakfast.

Ah! stamp not rudely on Hal Hudson's bed
Tho' oft he's stampt upon your nation's head;
For he was authorized, nay forced to do it,
Or else he'd been full sorely made to rue it—
Making a meal this good hat-maker died
And merrily, 'tis said, to his own Maker hied.

Messenger Monsey, M.D., 1788, aged 96.

Here lie my old limbs, my vexation now ends,
For I've lived much too long for myself and my friends ;
As for Churchyards and grounds which the parsons
    call Holy,
'Tis a rank piece of priestcraft and founded in folly ;
In short, I despise them ; and as for my soul,
Which may mount the last day with my bones from
    this Hole ;
I think that it really hath nothing to fear
From the God of mankind, whom I truly revere ;
What the next world may be, little troubles my pate ;
If not better than this, I beseech thee, oh ! Fate,
When the bodies of millions fly up in a riot
To let the old carcase of Monsey be quiet.

HANSLOPE.

Strong and athletic was my frame ;
Far from my native home I came,
And manly fought with Simon Byrne ;
Alas ! but liv'd not to return.

Reader, take warning by my fate,
Lest you should rue your case too late ;
If you have ever fought before,
Determine now to fight no more.

GAYTON, NORTHANTS. 1600.

On William Houghton.

Neere fourscore years have I tarryed
To this mother to be marryed ;
One wife I had, and children ten,
God bless the living, Amen, Amen.

Hutton.

In memory of
Donald Campbell, Esq. of Barbreek, N.B.
He died June 5th, 1801, aged 53 years. With
talents and a heart that might have rendered
him useful in Society in his career through life,
he unfortunately ran to the wrong side of the post,
and owing to peculiar circumstances, has experienced a good deal of worldly persecution, but
looks up to a merciful God (who always knows
our most inmost motives) for everlasting bliss.

Robert Sleath. Died 1805.
He kept the turnpike gate at Worcester, and
demanded toll from His Majesty, on his visit to
Bishop Hand and from this circumstance he was
known as " the man who stopped the King."

On Wednesday last old Robert Sleath
Passed through the turnpike gate of Death
To him would Death no toll abate,
Who stopped the King at Worcester gate.

St. Margaret's, Westminster. 1597.

In Parliament, a Burgess *Cole* was placed,
In *Westminster* the like for many years,
But now with Saints above his Soul is graced,
And lives a Burgess with Heav'ns Royal Peers.

Winchester College. 1541.

Beneath this stone shut up in the dark,
A fellow and a priest, yclep'd John Clark ;
With earthly rose-water he did delight ye,
But now he deals in heavenly *aqua vitæ*.

ALTON, HANTS.

> Fair Virtue's up old Time's the Auctioneer
> A lot so lovely can't be bought too dear,
> Be quick in your biddings ere you are too late,
> Time will not dwell, the hammer will not wait.

> 1814. *Joseph Jardan, Auctioneer.*

OLD MEN's HOSPITAL, NORWICH.

> In memory of Mrs. Phœbe Crewe
> who died May 28, 1817, aged 77 years.
> Who, during forty years
> practise as a midwife
> in this City, brought into
> the world nine thousand
> seven hundred and
> thirty children.

> Thomas Pyle. Died 1823. Aged 15.

> Here lies a son, whose tender life
>   To a mother's heart most dear,
> Bereft of life through wicked strife
>   Who once was all her care.

> By pugilism, a shameful sight,
>   To every mother's eyes,
> That dimmed the heavenly orbs of light,
>   Which forc'd convulsive cries.

> But still my hope shall ever be,
>   Though folly closed his life,
> That he's in heaven, from troubles free
>   From vanity and strife.

> Then let all youths a warning take
>   At his untimely fate,
> And call on God for mercy's sake,
>   Before it is too late.

At Walton-on-Thames.   Died 1842.   Aged 48.

William Maginn, L.L.D.

Here, early to bed, lies kind William Maginn,
Who with genius, wit, learning, Life's trophies to win,
Had neither great Lord nor rich cit of his kin,
Nor discretion to set himself up as to him ;
So his portion soon spent (like the poor heir of Lynn)
He turned author, ere yet there was beard on his chin,
And, whoever was out, or whoever was in,
For your Tories his fine Irish brains he would spin,
Who received prose and rhyme with a promising grin—
" Go ahead, you queer fish, and more power to
   your fin,"
But to stave from starvation stirred never a pin.
Light for long was his heart, tho' his breeches were thin,
Else his acting for certain, was equal to Quin ;
But at last he was beat, and sought help of the bin,
(All the same to the doctor from claret to gin),
Which led swiftly to gaol, and consumption therein.
It was much, when the bones rattled loose in the skin,
He got leave to die here—out of Babylon's din.
Barring drink and the girls, I ne'er heard a sin :
Many worse, better few, than bright broken Maginn.

J. G. Lockhart.

N.B.—Dr. Maginn is said to be the original of Thackeray's
" Captain Shandy."

On King Henry VIIIth's Jester.

Stay Traveller, guess who lies here :
I tell thee neither Lord nor Peer,
No Knight, no Gentleman of Note,
That boasts him of his antient Coate,
Which Herald's curiously emblazon,
For men (well skilled therein) to gaze on ;

Know then, that this was no such man
And I'll express him as I can :
He that beneath this Tombstone lies
Some called him Fool, some held him wise ;
For which, who better proof can bring,
Than to be favoured by a King :
And yet again, we may misdoubt him
A King hath always fools about him.
Is he more idiot than the rest
Who in a guarded coat can jest ?
Or can he wisdom's honour gain
That is all bravery, and no brain ?
Since no such things ; Wit truly bred,
I' th' Habit lies not, but i' th' Head.
But whether he was fool or knave,
He now lies sleeping in his grave,
Who never in his life found match,
Unless the Cardinal's fool call'd Patch :
Of whom some courtiers who did see
Them two alone, might say, *we three.*
And may be feared it is a phrase,
That may be used in these our days.
Well, more of him what should I say,
Both fools and wise men turn to clay ;
And this is all we have to trust,
That there's no difference in their dust ;
Rest quiet then beneath this Stone,
To whom late *Archy* was a Drone.

ALL HALLOWS, BREAD STREET.

Snow, the King's Trumpeter.

Thaw every breast, melt every eye with woe,
   Here's dissolution by the hand of Death !
To dirt, to water, turned the fairest Snow,
   O ! the King's trumpeter has lost his breath.

St. Bennet's.   1594.

Here lieth Katherine Prettyman
A mayde of seventeen yeeres,
In Suffolk born, in London bred,
As by her death appears.
With nature's gifts she was adorned,
Of honest birth and kin,
Her virtuous mind, with modest grace,
Did love of many win.
But when she should with honest match
Have liv'd a wedded life,
Stay there, quoth Jove, the world is nought,
For she shall be my wife.
And Death, since thou hast done thy due,
Lay nuptial rites aside,
And follow her into the grave,
That should have been your Bride ;
Whose honest life, and faithful end,
Her patience therewithal,
Doth plainly shew, that she with Christ,
Now lives, and ever shall.

Crich, Derbyshire.   *Circa* 1590.

On a family named Claye.

Souls they are made of Heavenly spirit :
From whence they come ye heavens inherite.
But know that bodyes made of Claye :
Death will devoure by night or daye
Yett is hee as hee was I saye :
He living and dead remayneth Claye.
His verye name that nature gave :
Is now as shalbe in his grave.
Tymes doth teache, experience tryes :
That Claye to duste the winde up dryes.
Then this a wonder compt wee must :
That want of wind should make Claye dust.

In a Churchyard at Chester.

On a crockery dealer.

> Beneath this stone lies Catherine Gray,
> Changed to a lifeless lump of clay ;
> By earth and clay she got her pelf,
> And now she's turned to earth herself.
> Ye weeping friends, let me advise,
> Abate your tears and dry your eyes ;
> For what avails a flood of tears ?
> Who knows but in a course of years,
> In some tall pitcher or brown pan,
> She in her shop may be again.

Battersea. 1613.

Hugh Morgan.

Sleepeth here in peace : whom men did late admire for worthful parts. To Queen Elizabeth he was chief 'pothecary, till her death.

> And in his science as he did excel
> In her high favour he always did dwell.
> To God religious, to all men kind,
> Frank to the poor, rich in content of mind.
> These were his virtues, in these died he,
> When he had liv'd an 100 years and 3.

Cannington.

> She to gain love did AMYable live,
> And Sara like to her Lord honour give ;
> Bare him ten children ; chastly bred them, free
> From superstition and impietie.
> Answer'd her worthy parents worth, and dyed
> A patterne to her sexe to shun vaine pride.

1621. *Amy St. Barbe, aged* 33.

UCKFIELD. 1610.

John Fuller.

Now I am dead and laid in grave,
And that my bones are rotten,
By this shall I remembered be,
Or else I am forgotten.

Someone has made a bull in imitating this in the Churchyard of Michaelchurch, Herts.

John Prosser is my name, and England is my nation.
Bowchurch is my dwelling place and Christ is my salvation.
Now I am dead and in my grave, and all my bones are rotten
As you pass by, remember me, when I am quite forgotten.

St. Mary Key, Ipswich. 1618.

Mary Cleere.

Cleere was my name, my life was also clear
Like name like life, for I the light did love
Earst that this life I left this did appear
Even unto men as unto God above.
Remit who did my sins, my fears remove
Ere that he call'd my soul to Christ my Love.

Norwich Cathedral. 1621.

William Inglott.

Here William Inglott, Organist doth rest,
Whose Art in Musick this Cathedral blest,
For Descant most, for Voluntary all,
He past on Organ, Song and Verginall.
He left this life at age of Sixty-seven,

And now 'mongst Angels sings in Heaven,
His Fame flies far, his Name shall never die,
See Art and Age here crown his memorie.

Other epitaphs to musicians are found. One dated
1645 is to the memory of William Lawes, killed at the
siege of West Chester.

Concord is conquered ; in this urn there lies
The Master of Great Musick's Mysteries ;
And in it is a riddle like the cause
Will Lawes was slain by those whose Wills were Lawes.

AT NORWICH. 1669.
On Richard Yleward.

Here lyes a perfect Harmonie
Of Truth and Faith and Loyaltie,
And whatsoever Vertues can,
Be reckoned up, was in this man,
His sacred ashes here abide,
Who in God's service lived and died.
But now by Death advanced higher,
To serve in the Celestial Quire.
    God Save the King.

AT KIMBERLEY. 1678.
        John Jenkins.   Aged 86.

Under this stone rare Jenkins lye
The Master of the Musick Art,
Whom from the Earth, the God on high,
Called up to him, to bear his Part.
Aged 86.   October 27
In Anno 78, He went to Heaven.

In Llanfilantwthyl Churchyard.

Under this stone lies Meredith Morgan,
Who blew the bellows of our Church Organ ;
Tobacco he hated, to smoke most unwilling,
Yet never so pleased as when pipes he was filling ;
No reflection on him for rude speech could be cast,
Tho' he gave our old organist many a blast.

No puffer was he
Tho' a capital blower ;
He could fill double G
And now lies a note lower.

Bluntsham. 1621.

On a wrestler.

Here lies the Conqueror conquered,
Valiant as ever England bred ;
Whom neither art, nor steel, nor strength
Could e'er subdue, till death at length
Threw him on his back, ﹁nd here he lyes
In hopes hereafter to arise.

Her' rest gives me a rest less life
Because she was a virtuous wife ;
But yet I rest in hopes to see
That daye of Christ and then see thee.

James Barker. 1622. Aged 44.

St. Peter's, Oxford.

Here lyeth Dr. Rawlinson's two younger daughters ;
Elizabeth, who died May 21, 1624, and Dorothy,
who died Jan 10, 1629.

Two little sisters lie under this stone
Their Mothers were two, their Fathers but one.
At 5 years old departed the younger,

The elder lived 9 years 5 days and no longer.
Learn hence ye young gallants to cast away laughter,
As soon comes the lamb as the sheep to the slaughter.

NORWICH.

My time is short, the longer is my rest
God calls them soonest whom he loves the *Best*.

1629. *Henry Best.*

Many other punning epitaphs belong to this date.

AT ST. GILES', HERTS. 1631.
Anne Poure.

Pour, Rich was in the spirit
Anne Poure, Rich Poure by Christ's merit.

ST. AUGUSTINE'S.
(On a brass plate) Wm. Lamb.
Oh! Lamb of God! which sin didn't take away,
And as a Lamb was offered up for sin,
Where I poor Lamb, went from thy flock astray
Yet Thou O Lord vouchsafe thy Lamb to win
Home to thy flock, and hold thy Lamb therein.
That at the day when Lambs and Goats shall sever
Of thy choice Lambs, *Lamb* may be one for ever.

SOUTHWOLD.
Thomas Gardiner,
Historian of Southwold and Denwich, buried
with his two wives, Honor and Virtue.

Between Honor and Virtue, here doth lie
The remains of Old Antiquity.

Low Leyton.

Elizabeth Wood.

Wail not, my Wood, thy Trees untimely fall,
They were but Leaves that Autumn's blast could spoil ;
The Bark bound up, and some fair Fruit withal,
Transplanted only, she exchanged her soil,
She is not dead, she did but fall to rise
And leave the *Woods* to live in Paradise.

Peebles.

Thos. Hope and Children.

Here lie three Hopes enclosed within
Death's prisoners by Adam's sin,
Yet rest in hope that they shall be
Set by the second Adam free.

Elstree.

This extraordinary effusion is on a wife named **Olive**.

Behold and know how heaven is repossest
Of her sweet soul whose corps interred doth rest
Near to this place ; for silence would her wrong
If that my Muse had not addrest this song
Of sacred trophies in her vertuous praise,
Which cannot die, but must survive always.
A fruitful peaceful *Olive* was her name,
So was her Life, her Death, her Faith the same ;
Emblem'd by Dove with Olive leaf in bill
Which show'd glad Noah God had done his will,
And forc'd the swelling Deluge Flood resort
To channels low, in bank, in bounds their port ;
This *Olive* lived much more content with me,
Than did this Dove, good Noah, in ark with thee,

And brought me Olive branch to glad my heart,
As Dove rejoiced, the ceasing floating part,
And then with ghost did penetrate the skies
More high than Dove, beyond object of eyes ;
Her heart, her mind, her Soul, and Faith most pure,
Were link't in Christ so stedfast and so sure,
As helped her soul more high than Dove could flie,
Now therefore Noah, thy Dove I must pass by ;
Mounting the heavens by wings of faith
Her soul's aspect discharged of sin and pain ;
Where hope assures and puts me out of doubt
That this late *Olive* mine is round about,
Beset with God's favour and mercy seat,
And with his love of all his joys for meat,
Which power shall adamantine wise restore
Her corps to suit which clad her soul before.
Dignified, glorified, eternized
Sanctified at last, as first baptized.

IN BUCKS.

On a Shepherd named Faithful.

> Faithful lived and Faithful died,
> Faithful shepherded on the hill-side—
> The hills so wide, the fields surround,
> In the day of judgment he'll be found.

GATESHEAD, DURHAM.

On a Newcastle architect.

> Here lies Robert Trollope,
> Who made yon stones roll up :
> When death took his soul up
> His body filled this hole up.

St. Maire's, Sandwich.

My resting road is found
Vain hope and hap adieu,
Love whom you list
Death hath me rid from you.
The Lord did me from London bring
To lay my body close herein
I was my father's only heir,
And the first my mother bare.
But before one year was spent
The Lord his messenger for me sent.

1635. Robert Needler.

In the North Chapel, outside the Priest's Door, Kingsbridge Church, Devon, is to be found the following epitaph in memory of : " Robert, commonly called Bone (due to he being the chief parish gravedigger), Phillip died 1795."

Here lie I at the Chapel door,
Here lie I because I'm poor,
The farther in the more you'll pay,
Here lie I as warm as they.

An interesting subject of research is that of various tradesmen's epitaphs scattered up and down the country. Here is one from Upton-on-Severn.

Beneath this stone in hopes of Zion
Doth lie the landlord of the Lion ;
His son keeps on the business still,
Resigned unto the heavenly will.

Briefer still is the inscription over the grave of a departed hostler, to be found in Frodsham Churchyard.

Here is Lays,
Killed by a chaise.

In the Churchyard of St. Mary, Cheltenham, may be seen a flat stone to the memory of John Higgs, pig-killer.

> Here lies John Higgs,
> A famous man for killing pigs,
> For killing pigs was his delight,
> Both morning, afternoon, and night,
> Both heats and colds he did endure,
> Which no physician could e'er cure.
> His knife is laid, his work is done ;
> I hope to heaven his soul is gone.

In an old Fifeshire churchyard is said to be the following.

> Here lies my gude and gracious Auntie
> Whom Death has packed in his portmanty.

Another absurdity is the well-meaning, but unfortunately expressed, inscription on another Scottish tombstone.

> Erected to the memory of
> John MacFarlane
> Drowned in the Water of Leith
> By a few affectionate friends.

BERKELEY, GLOUCESTERSHIRE.

> Here lies the Duke of Suffolk's fool,
>   Men called him Dickey Pearce ;
> His folly served to make folks laugh
>   When wit and mirth were scarce.
> Poor Dick, alas ! is dead and gone,
>   What signifies to cry,
> Dickeys enough are still behind
>   To laugh at by-and-by.
> Buried 18 of June, MDCCXXVIII.
> My Lord that's gone made himself much sport of him.
>
> *Swift.*

BELTURBET, IRELAND.

Here lies John Higley, whose father and mother were drowned in their passage from America; had they both lived they would have been buried here.

One sometimes wonders when noting a quaintly-worded epitaph on a time-worn tombstone, whether our descendents will find the twentieth century memorials an interesting field for research. Somehow the modern inscriptions seem to lack the pleasant spontaneity, the good, human ring which is so refreshing to discover in the older ones. Doubtless ours is a sterner philosophy. It was no dour cynic who inscribed above a Hertfordshire bricklayer these lines :

> Silent in dust lies mould'ring here
> A Parish Clerk of voice most clear ;
> None Joseph Rogers could excel
> In laying bricks or singing well.

There is a glint of humour, too—of a different kind, and possibly unintentional—in this from Oxted Parish Church : " Let this patterne of piety, mapp of misery, mirrour of patience, here rest." But for deliberate irony we must go to the sly fellow who cut in stone above his friend the short suggestive words : " John Burns."

ROCHDALE, LANCS.

" Tim Bobbin's Grave "
(John Collier, 1786)

> Here lies John, and with him Mary,
> Cheek by jowl, and never vary ;
> No wonder that they so agree,
> John wants no punch, and Moll no tea.

ALSTON, CUMBERLAND.

> Here lies poor Jones,
> Who all his life collected bones ;
> But death, that great and grisly spectre,
> That most amazing bone collector,
> Hath boned poor Jones, so neat and tidy,
> That here he lies in bona-fide.

BANGOR.

> Poor Martha Snell, her's gone away,
> Her would if her could, but her couldn't stay,
> Her had two bad legs and a badish cough,
> But her legs it was that carried her off.

BEDWELTY, NEAR TREDEGAR.

On the Tombstone of a Wife.

This poor man wept and the Lord heard him and delivered him out of all his troubles.

PEWSEY, WILTS.

> Here lies the Body of
> Lady o' Looney.
> Great niece of Burke
> commonly called the Sublime.
> She was
> Bland, Passionate, and deeply Religious,
> also she painted in water colours
> and sent several pictures
> to the exhibition.
> She was first cousin
> to Lady Jones
> and of such
> is the Kingdom of Heaven.

Dundee.

>Here lies John, late Mayor of Dundee,
>Here lies Him, here lies He,
>A. B. C. E. F. G.
>Di Do Dum, Di, Do, Dee.

St. Michael's, Aberystwyth.

To memory of a young man, a hosier, near Nottingham, who had a sweetheart named Hannah.

>He left his hose, his Hannah, and his love
>To sing Hosannahs in the world above.

Bideford.

>Here lies the Landlord of " The Lion,"
>His hopes removed to lands of Sion,
>His wife, resigned to Heaven's will,
>Will carry on the business still.

>(Two Years Later)
>Here lies the Landlord's loving wife,
>Her soul removed from lands of strife.
>She's gone aloft her spouse to tell
>The Inn he left her turned out well.

The Isle of Wight.

Here lies the body of William Smith of London, who came here and died for the benefit of his health.

Ulster.

>Erected to the Memory of
>John Phillips
>Accidentally Shot
>As a mark of affection by his brother.

GRANTHAM.

> John Palfreyman, who is buried here,
> Was aged four and twenty year,
> And near this place his body lies ;
> Likewise his father—when he dies.

> In memory of ——
> who died of cholera morbus,
> caused by eating green fruit
> In the certain hope of a
> blessed immortality
> Reader, go thou & do likewise.

BUNHILL FIELDS.

> Here lies
> Dame Mary Page
> Relect of Sir Gregory Page, Bart.
> She departed this life
> March 4, 1728
> aged 56.
> In 67 months she was tapped
> 66 times.   Had taken
> away from her 240 gallons of
> water—without ever repining
> at her case.
> Of such is the Kingdom of Heaven.

Also another, which is interesting as an example of killing two birds with one epitaph, is from Bideford Church.

> Here lies the body of Sarah Sexton,
> She was a wife that never vexed one.
> I can't say as much for her on the next stone.

HOLMER, HEREFORD.

A virtuous woman is 5s to her husband.   (" A crown " was meant, but the mason had not space.)

COLERNE, WILTSHIRE.

In memory of
Jonathan Southward,
Butcher, who
died, February 19th, 1727.
Aged 37.
Also Thomas Southward
Butcher, who
died April 16, 1777
Aged 60.

By these inscriptions, be it understood,
My occupation was in shedding blood,
And many a beast by me was weekly slain,
Hunger to ease, and mortals to maintain.
Now here I rest from sin and sorrow free,
By means of Him who shed his blood for me.

From a Cheshire tombstone of John Webb, landlord
of the Red Lion.

In life a jovial sot was he,
He died from inebriete.
A cup of burnt canary sack,
To Earth from Heaven would bring him back.

While that of a young baby from Somersetshire is also
distinctly quaint.

Here am I, the last of seven,
And yet the first to enter Heaven.

From St. Pancras, London, on the grave of a Mr. Talbot.

Here lies—believe it if you can—
Who though a lawyer was an honest man ;
To him the gates of heaven shall open wide !
And quickly close 'gainst all the tribe beside !

The following epitaph on a railway porter is distinctly neat.

> He climbed the dizzy steepes of Heaven
>   Through peril, toil and pain,
> O God to us may grace be given
>   To follow in " the train."

The following epitaph on an old lady is said to be original.

> Constance Bevon, wife of John
> Lies beneath this marble stone ;
> Fat and busom, round and stout,
> 'Twas apoplexy bowled her out.

St. Agnes, Cornwall.

> Here lies the body of Joan Carthew,
> Born at St. Columb, died at St. Cue ;
> Children she had five,
> Three are dead and two alive ;
> Those that are dead choosing rather
> To die with their mother than live with their father !

Jersey.

To a Brewer.

> Here lies poor Burton,
>   He was both hale and stout ;
> Death laid him on his bitter bier,
>   Now in another world he hops about.

Another epitaph on a fat woman.

> " All flesh is grass,"
> The Scriptures they do say,
> And grass when dead
> Is turnèd into hay.
> Now when the reapers her away do take,
> Moi what a wopping haystack she will make.

SPARTA, CALIFORNIA.

In memory ov
John Smith, who met
wierlent death near this spot,
18 hunderd and 40 too.   He was shot
by his own pistill.
It was not one of the new kind,
but a old-fashioned
brass barrel, and of such is the
Kingdom of Heaven.

Honest lawyers must indeed be rare !   Here is an inscription on a tomb in Pelynt Church, Cornwall, on the grave of Edward Trelawney, barrister.

Oh ! what a bubble, vapour, puff of breath,
A nest of worms, a lump of pallid earth,
Is mud-walled man !   Before we mount on high
We cope with change, we wander after day.
Here lyes an honest lawyer, wot you what
A thing for all the world to wonder at !

This turf has drank a
Widow's tear ;
Three of her husbands
Slumber here.

A Bitter Memory.

Some time ago it was reported that Mr. G. Winch was chairman at a dinner given by a Maidstone brewing firm. In merry mood he suggested his own epitaph.

G. Winch, the Brewer, lies buried here,
In life he was both h-ale and stout ;
Death brought him to his bitter bier ;
Now in Heaven he hops about.

MONTROSE. 1757.

Here lyes—the *bodeys* of George Young and Isabel Guthrie
and all *their posterity* for
more than fifty years backward.

The following epitaph is alleged to be on a country
parson's grave.

The horse bit the parson,
    How came that to pass ?
The horse heard the parson say,
    All flesh is grass.

The following epitaph is said to be seen at Sunderland.

Here lies the body of Andrew Gear,
Whose mouth did stretch from ear to ear ;
Stranger, step lightly o'er his head,
For if he gapes, by Josh, you're dead.

Monumental masons have sometimes amusing experiences.
One relates that being requested by the disconsolate weeping
widow of one of his late fellow townsmen to place on the
slab of her dear departed the words : " My sorrow is greater
than I can bear," he took care to space the sentence so
that room was left for an addition.

A few months later she called to inquire how much it
would cost to efface the inscription and substitute another.

" No need of that, marm," he answered soothingly,
" you see there's jes' room to add ' alone.' "

Here lies John Wood, that good old man,
    We ne'er shall see him more ;
He used to wear a long blue coat
    All buttoned down before.

While the old churchyard of Rhayader, in Radnorshire, was being demolished, some years ago, a tombstone was unearthed which bore the following " in memoriam " verse.

> I plant these shrubs upon your grave, dear wife,
> That something on this spot may boast of life.
> Shrubs must wither and all earth must rot ;
> Shrubs may revive : but you, thank heaven, will not.

This is reported from Monmouthshire, in which county the following is inscribed on a single-slab stone stile into the graveyard at Llanvair Discoed :

> Whoever heres on Sonday
>   Will practis playing at ball,
> It may be before Monday
>   The Devil will have you all.

The sad end of Mary Ann Lowder is told in her epitaph in Burlington Churchyard :

> Here lies the body of Mary Ann Lowder,
> She burst while drinking a seidlitz powder,
> Called from this world to her heavenly rest,
> She should have waited till it effervesced.

Dr. Kaye, medical officer for the West Riding of Yorkshire, some time ago spoke about the folly of tight lacing, and quoted the following epitaph, entitled " Mary's Little Corset " :

> Mary had a little waist,
>   She laced it smaller still ;
> A stone o'er Mary has been placed
>   Out on the silent hill.

> And on that stone these words are writ,
>   " Oh, let us hope she's gone,
> " Where angels never care a bit
>   " 'Bout what they have got on."

Those who are rash in removing their heavy flannels too early in the spring may learn wisdom from the fate of Uncle Peter Daniels, as described on his tombstone in an American town.

> Beneath this stone, a lump of clay,
> Lies Uncle Peter Dan'els,
> Who, early in the month of May,
> Took off his winter flannels.

Another American epitaph is suggestive.

> Beneath this plain pine board is lying
> The body of Joshua Hight,
> " Cheer up," the parson told him, dying ;
> " Your future's very bright."

> Slowly the sick man raised his head,
> His weeping friends amazing.
> " Parson, it's most too bright," he said,
> " For I can see it blazing ! "

Two more Transatlantic epitaphs. The first, in a Nevada burial ground, runs : " Sacred to the memory of Hank Monk, the Whitest, Biggest-hearted, and Best Stage-driver of the West, who was Kind to All, Thought Ill of None. He lived in a Strange Era, and was a Hero ; and the Wheels of his Coach are now Ringing on Golden Streets." The second also belongs to the Far West : " To Lem S. Frame, who during his life shot 89 Indians, whom the Lord delivered into his hands, and who was looking forward to making up his hundred before the end of the year, when he fell asleep in Jesus at his house at Hawk's Ferry, March 27, 1843.

Two ladies were discussing their debts. Said one : " I can't pay a single bill. If I died to-morrow two words would make me a suitable epitaph : ' Account rendered.' " " Oh, said the other, " one word would be enough for me : ' Settled.' "

M

The following is over the grave of a man who grew rich
selling fertilizers to farmers.

> Six feet beneath
> This funeral wreath
> Is laid upon the shelf
> One Jerry Jones,
> Who dealt in bones,
> And now he's bones himself.

A familiar epitaph, which may be new to some readers,
deals with the domestic servant question.

> Here lies a poor woman who was always tired,
> She lived in a house where help wasn't hired :
> Her last words on earth were : " Dear friends, I am going
> To where there's no cooking, or washing, or sewing,
> For everything there is exact to my wishes,
> For where they don't eat there's no washing of dishes,
> I'll be where loud anthems will always be ringing,
> But having no voice I'll be quit of the singing,
> Don't mourn for me now, don't mourn for me never,
> I am going to do nothing for ever and ever."

There was a humorous doctor, rejoicing in the name of
I. Letsome, who composed his own epitaph in the following
terms.

> When people's ill they come to I,
>   I physics, bleeds, and sweats 'em ;
> Sometimes they live, sometimes they die ;
>   What's that to I ?   I Letsome.

This is a reflection on the fair fame of the leading
Gloucestershire health resort.

> Here I lie with my three daughters,
> Who died drinking Chelt'nam waters.
> If we had stuck to Epsom Salt,
> We should not sleep in this cold vault.

How many visitors to Winchester Cathedral have ever seen the tomb of the Hampshire Grenadier who died through drinking small beer on a hot day. In the graveyard is a tombstone to the memory of Thomas Thetcher, a Grenadier in the Hants Militia, who died "of a violent fever contracted by drinking small beer when hot on the 12th May, 1764." The verse underneath runs :—

> Here sleeps in peace a Hampshire grenadier,
> Who caught his death by drinking cold small beer,
> Soldiers be wise from his untimely fall,
> And when you're hot drink strong or not at all.

The stone was restored in 1781 by the officers of the garrison, who subscribed the following lines :—

> An honest soldier never is forgot,
> Whether he die by musket or by pot.

On the grave of a miser and his wife who did not wish to have much money spent on their epitaphs. When the husband died all that was written on the tomb was :—

> Thorp's Corps.

And later, when his wife joined him, it was changed to

> Here Lieth Thorpses Corpses.

The following epitaph is from Pinner on Lord Coningsby, who, in 1715, impeached Harley, Earl of Oxford, of "high treason and other crimes and misdemeanours."

> Here lies Lord Coningsby : be civil,
> The rest God knows—perhaps the Devil.

A genuine epitaph on twin babies from a Welsh Churchyard.

> We tasted of life's bitter cup,
> Refused to drink the portion up,
> We turned our little heads aside,
> Disgusted with the taste—and died.

Then there is the clever but too familiar " Epitaph on a Baby One Month Old " :—

> Since I am so quickly done for,
> I wonder what I was begun for.

A variation of the same theme is :—

> Oped my eyes, took a peep ;
> Didn't like it, went to sleep.

Being " unspotted of the world," Miss Binn—was apparently also of tender years.

> Here lies the body of Betsy Binn,
> Who was so very pure within,
> She burst her outer shell of sin,
> And hatched herself a cherubim.

There is a strong smack of Catullus about Thomas Hardy's " Epitaph on a Pessimist," printed in a recent number of the *London Mercury*.

> " I'm Smith of Stoke, aged sixty odd,
> I've lived without a dame
> From youth-time on : and would to God
> My dad had done the same."

Here lies Will Smith—and, what's something rarish, He was born, bred, and hanged, all in the same parish.

A quaint epitaph from Wrotham churchyard.

> He gave to none designed offence,
> Honi soit qui mal y pense.

And a famous one in Kensal Green, over the grave of the great French cook.

> " Soyer Tranquille."

Epitaph on the tombstone of Dr. Fuller :—

> Here lies " Fuller's earth."

The following have a distinctly American flavour.

Oh ! weep for little Johnny, who
    Has gone to his repose,
His eyes were such a lovely blue,
    His cheeks were like the rose.
Though his departure grieves us much,
    We must not show contrition,
For shall we grudge the angels such
    A valuable addition ?

Here lie the bones of Matthew Jones,
Who in his lifetime collected Bones ;
But Death, that grizly boney Spectre,
That all amazing Bone Collector,
Has boned poor Jones so nice and tidy,
That here he lies quite bonafide !

Little Willy in the best of sashes,
Played with fire and was burnt to ashes !
Very soon the room got chilly,
But *no one* liked to poke poor Willie !

Be not afraid to venture near this stone !
Of naught contagious did she die,
The maid who rests beneath this stone
She died of " constancy " alone.

Here lies John Bun,
He was killed by a gun,
His name was not Bun, but Wood,
But Wood would not rhyme with gun, but Bun would.

Mary Anne has gone to rest,
Safe at last on Abraham's breast,
Which may be nuts for Mary Anne,
But is certainly rough on Abraham.

Mary Lee, only three,
Hung her harp on the willow tree.
Singular that she should be
Tall enough to reach that tree.

Little Willie from his mirror
  Licked the mercury right off,
Thinking, in his childish error,
  It would cure the whooping cough.
At the funeral his mother
  Smartly said to Mrs. Brown :
" 'Twas a chilly day for Willie
When the mercury went down."

This is the last long resting-place of dear Jemimer's
  bones ;
Her soul ascended into space amidst our tears and
  groans.
She was not pleasing to the eye, nor had she any brain,
And when she talked 'twas through her nose, which
  gave her friends much pain.
But still we feel that she was worth the money that
  was spent
Upon the coffin and the hearse (the mourning plumes
  were lent).

Here lies my wife,
Here let her lie.
She's at rest,
And so am *I.*

Here lies Elizabeth Wise,
Who died of thunder sent from Heaven,
In 1777.

When dear papa went up to Heaven,
　　What grief mamma endured ;
And yet that grief was softened, for
　　Papa he was insured.

His body lies this stone beneath
　　Whose lies the Press did fill ;
The ruling passion's strong in death,
　　For here he's lying still.

Forgive, blest shade, the crocodile tear
　　Which, with an obvious effort, mourns thy flight ;
From out a world of critics too severe,
　　Who treat thee must less kindly than they might.

It may be that a future age more kind,
　　May disinter thy works—who could have missed 'em,
And for the same a *raison d'etre* find,
　　In some ingenious hidden cypher system.

Collisions sore, three, four, she bore
　　Physicians wor in vain,
For old and rusted the biler busted
　　And smashed the excursion train.
　　" Her end was pieces."

Ireland, of course, is the happy hunting ground for epitaphs, as the following from an Irish churchyard shows:—

Here lie the remains of John Hall, grocer,
The world is not worth a *fig*, and I have good *raisins*
　　for saying so.

Yet another (from Larchfield) :—

Under this stone lie two babies dear,
One is buried in *Connaught*, and *t'other here.*

And a third :—

> Within this grave do lie,
> Back to back, my wife and I ;
> When the last trump the air shall fill,
> If she gets up, I'll just lie still.

And, lastly, an epitaph on a dentist, which is distinctly good :—

> Stranger !   Approach this spot with gravity !
> John Brown is filling his last cavity.

In a small country church near New York—West Chester county to be exact—is a tombstone inscribed to the memory of a little girl who died at the age of seven. The epitaph is beautifully simple :—

> She done her best.

On Grimaldi (the famous clown).

> " Here I am ! "

In a Staffordshire Churchyard.

> Here lies father and mother and sister and I,
>   We all died within the space of one short year,
> They all be buried at Wimble, except I,
>   And I be buried here.

" Tears cannot restore him, therefore I weep," is a good one, but the following pithy epitaph on the tomb of a doctor (given me by a medical man) comes near it :—

> He survived all his patients.

At Staverton.

> Here lieth the body of Betty Cowden
> Who would live longer but she couden ;
> Sorrow and grief made her decay,
> Till her bad leg carried her away.

The following one, copied at Fowey Churchyard in Cornwall, and dated 1664, is decidedly curious and has a hint of a story about it :—

> Reader here lies—but forbear
> To read more without a tear,
> One—I cannot speak the rest,
> You may weep. I'll smite my breast,
> Grief preventing, and this stone,
> Too small to be written on.
> Only this—a spotless maid,
> Sarah—in Abram's bosom's laid.

Minster, a little village near Queenborough.

> Here interred George Anderson doth lie
> By falling on an anchor he did die
> In Sheerness Yard on Good Friday
> Ye 6th of April, I do say
> All you that read my Allegy ; be always
> Ready for to die—aged 42 years.

> Here lies Tom Hyde ;
> It's a pity that he died ;
> We had rather
> If it had been his father ;
> If it had been his sister,
> We had not missed her ;
> If the whole generation,
> It had been better for the nation.

Quoted in letter July 9th, 1667, as an epitaph composed on the death of a son of Lord Chancellor Hyde.

Epitaph on an atheist.

> Beneath this stone bereft of breath,
>   And freed from mortal strife,
> Lies one who living, feared not death,
>   Nor dying, hoped for life.

From Bakewell Churchyard, Derby.

> The vocal powers let us mark
> Of Philip, our late parish clerk;
> In Church one never heard a layman
> With a clearer voice say Amen:
> Who now with Hallelujah's sound
> Like him can make the roofs rebound?
> The choir lament his choral tones
> The town so soon—here lies his bones.

On a Marine Officer.

> Here lies retired from busy scenes
> A First Lieutenant of Marines;
> Who lately lived in peace and plenty
> On board the ship the Atalanta:
> Now, stripped of all his warlike show,
> And laid in box of elm below,
> Confined to earth in narrow borders
> He rises not till further orders.

At Loch Ransa.

> Here lies Donald and his wife
> Janet MacFee:
> Aged 40 he
> And 30 she.

On a Mr. Bywater.

> Here lie the remains of his relative's pride
> Bywater he lived, and by water he died;
> Though by water he fell, yet by water he'll rise
> By water baptismal attaining the skies.

On a Miser.

> Here lies one who for medicine would not give
> A little gold, and so his life he lost:
> I fancy now he'd wish to live again
> Could he but guess how much his funeral cost.

On the south wall of Streatham Church :—

Elizabeth, wife of Major-General Hamilton, who was married forty-seven years, and never did *one* thing to disoblige her husband.

An epitaph from a tombstone in the Naval Cemetery, English Harbour, Antigua, W.I. :—

Sacred to the memory of Thomas Wotton, A.B., aged 34, who was accidentally killed in the execution of his duty on board H.M.S. " Phaeton," July 28th, 1863.

> A noble fellow there he stood,
> With 10 years' service " Very good,"
> A seaman's pride to firmly make
> The bowsprit all its strain partake.
> A block it split, and sprung in two,
> The angry fragments round him flew ;
> One struck poor Wotton's manly head
> And left him bleeding, dying, dead.
> He's gone from us, he's gone from sight,
> But God is good, His judgment right.
> The just he takes, the sinner lives,
> He loves us all, and all forgives.

To Ann Short (an acrostic).

> Who said : " I am short of everything."

> Am short, O Lord, of praising thee
> Nothing I can do right ;
> Needy and naked, poor I be,
> Short, Lord I am of sight !
> How short I am of love and grace !
> Of everything I'm short !
> Renew me, then I'll follow place
> Through good and bad report.

The writer of the above was David Love, a well-known character in Nottingham, on whose gravestone the following epitaph was written on his death in 1821.

> Here rests his head upon the lap of earth,
> A minstrel old in Nottingham well-known,
> In Caledonia was his humble birth
> But England makes his aged bones her own.
> Long were his verses, and his life was long,
> Wide, as a recompense, his fame was spread ;
> He sold for halfpence (all he had) a song,
> He earned by them ('twas all he wished) his bread.
> No further I his merits can disclose,
> His ardour dwells where David late abode,
> Go, buy his life, wrote by himself, which shows
> His service to his country, and his God.

At Hindhead, Surrey, there is or was the following memorial :—

> This Stone
> was erected in detestation of a barbarous
> Murder
> Committed near this spot
> on an
> Unknown Sailor
> by Edward Lonogan, Michael Casey
> and James Marshall
> September 24th, 1786
> Gen. ix-6.
> " Whoso sheddeth man's blood shall
> his blood be shed."

The murderers were hung and gibbeted on the spot. In 1827 the Trustees of the Turnpike Road offered a reward of ten guineas for the discovery of " the evil disposed person or persons who did maliciously break, deface, or injure the stone," the announcement appearing in a Portsmouth paper.

A monumental inscription in the churchyard of Grimmingham, Norfolk.

Sacred
to the memory of
Thomas Jackson, Comedian,
who was engaged 21st of Dec. 1741, to play a
comic cast of character, in this great theatre
the World; for many of which he was
prompted by nature to excel.

The season being ended, his benefit over,
the charges all paid, and his account closed,
he made his exit in the tragedy of Death, on
the 17th of March, 1798, in full assurance of
being called once more to rehearsal; where
he hopes to find his forfeits all cleared, his
cast of parts bettered, and his situation made
agreeable, by him who paid the great stock-
debt, for the love he bore to performers
in general.

SUSSEX.

Here lie two children
By water confounded,
One died of dropsy
T'other was drownded.

Here lies a Peck which some men say
Was first of all a Peck of clay;
This, wrought by skill divine while fresh
Became a curious Peck of flesh.
Through various forms its Maker ran,
Then, adding breath, made Peck a man.
Full fifty years Peck felt life's bubbles,
Till death relieved a Peck of troubles.
Then fell poor Peck, as all things must,
And here he lies, a Peck of dust.

TETBURY.

In a vault underneath lie interred several of the Saunderses, late of this parish. Particulars the last day will disclose. Amen.

TAIBACH, SOUTH WALES.

Hurrah, my boys ! at the Parson's fall,
For if he'd lived he'd a buried us all.
Poems and epitaphs are but stuff ;
Here lies Bob Barras—and that's enough.

FULHAM.

Ye who possess the brightest charms of life,
A tender friend—a kind indulgent wife,
Oh, learn their worth ! In her beneath this stone
These pleasing attributes together shone.
Was not true happiness with them combined ?
Ask of the spoil'd being she has left behind.
                                    He's gone too.

ST. OLAVE'S, SOUTHWARK.

On Mr. Munday.

Hallowed be the Sabaoth,
    And farewell all worldly Pelfe ;
The Weeke begins on Tuesday,
    For Munday hath hang'd himself.

LILLINGTON, KENILWORTH.

Cottons and muslins all adieu,
    And cambrics, too, farewell—
Plain, striped, and figured, old and new,
    Three-quarters, yard, or ell.
By nail and yard I've measured ye
    As customers inclined—
The churchyard now has measured me
    And nails my coffin bind.

Truro.

> Here lies we
> Babies three.
> Here we must lie
> Until the Lord do cry,
> " Come out and live wi' I."

St. Petrock's Church, Lydford, Devon.

Here lies in horizontal position the outside case of George Routleigh, watchmaker, whose abilities in that line were an honour to his profession—integrity was the mainspring, and prudence the regulator of all the actions of his life. Humane, generous, and liberal, his hand never stopped till he had relieved distress. So nicely regulated were all his movements that he never went wrong, except when set agoing by people who did not know his key; even then he was easily set right again. He had the art of disposing his time so well that the hours glided away in one continued round of pleasure and delight, till an unlucky moment put a a period to his existence. He departed this life November 14, 1802, aged fifty-seven. Wound up in hopes of being taken in hand by his Maker and being thoroughly cleansed, repaired, and set agoing in the world to come.

All Saints', Leighton Buzzard.

> Cease weeping, parents, 'twas my Maker's will
> That I should fall by lightning in the field.
> At God's command it struck, and then I fell :
> I had not time to bid my friends farewell.
> My Father ran, though he could scarcely stand,
> When he saw me lay burning on the land ;
> And with his hand he put the fire out,
> Saying, dear Lord, my son is dead, I doubt.

ROCHDALE. 1748.

On a Sexton.

> Here lies Jo Green, who arch has been,
>   And drove a grinful trade
> With powerful Death, till out of breath,
>   He threw away his spade.
> When Death beheld his comrade yield,
>   He, like a cunning knave,
> Came soft as wind, poor Jo behind,
>   And pushed him to his grave.
> Reader ! hast thou one tear in store,
> Weep, since Jo's tongue can wag no more.

CANTERBURY.

> Sacred to the memory of two sisters dear,
> One lies at Margate and t'other here.

WEYBRIDGE CHURCHYARD.

> As careful mothers doth to sleeping lay
> The child that doth too long the wanton play,
> So, to avoid my youth's approaching crimes,
> Nature, my nurse, layed me to bed betimes.

BIDEFORD CHURCHYARD.

> Here lies the Hope of a fond Mother
> And the Blasted expectations of a disappointed Father.

> The wedding day appointed was
> And wedding clothes provided,
> But ere that day did come, alas !
> He sickened and he die did.

PRESTONPANS CHURCHYARD.

> William Mathieson here lies,
>   Whose age was forty-one ;
> February 17 he dies,
>   Went Isbel Mitchell from,
> Who was his married wife,
> The fourth part of his life.
> The soul it cannot die
>   Though the body be turned to clay.
> Yet meet again they must,
>   At the last day
> Trumpets shall sound, archangels cry,
>   Come forth Isbel Mitchell
> And meet Will Mathieson in the sky !

MOULTON, CAMBRIDGESHIRE.

Sacred to the Memory of Lettuce Manning.

> Oh, cruel death
>   To satisfy thy palate,
> Cut down our Lettuce
>   To make a salad.

RIBBESFORD, BEWDLEY.

On the Wife of the Parish Clerk.

> The children of Israel wanted bread,
>   And the Lord he sent them manna,
> Old clerk Wallace wanted a wife,
>   And the Devil he sent him Anna.

GREAT TORRINGTON, DEVON.

> Here lies a man who was killed by lightning ;
> He died when his prospects seemed to be brightening.
> He might have cut a flash in this world of trouble,
> But the flash cut him, and he lies in the stubble.

N

GLOUCESTER.

> Beneath this dust lies the smouldering crust
> Of Eleanor Batchelor Shoven,
> Well versed in the arts of pies, puddings, and tarts
> And the lucrative trade of the oven.
>
> When she'd lived long enough
> She made her last puff,
> A puff by her husband much praised,
> And now she doth lie and makes a dirt pie
> And hopes that her crust will be raised.

CLIFTON, GLOUCESTERSHIRE.

On John Hippisley.

> When the Stage heard that Death had struck her John,
> Gay Comedy her Sables first put on ;
> Laughter lamented that her Fav'rite died,
> And Mirth herself ('tis strange) laid down and cry'd.
> Wit drooped his head, e'en Humour seemed to mourn,
> And solemnly sat pensive o'er his urn.

WOOLWICH CHURCHYARD.

Sacred to the memory of Major James Brush, Royal Artillery, who was killed by the accidental discharge of a pistol by his orderly, 14th April, 1831. Well done, good and faithful servant.

OXFORD.

Merideth.

> Here lies one blown out of breath,
> Who lived a merry life, and died a Merideth.

Corby Churchyard, Lincolnshire.

On an Auctioneer.

> Beneath this stone, facetious wight,
> Lies all that's left of poor Joe Wright.
> Few heads with knowledge more informed,
> Few hearts with friendship better warmed.
> With ready wit and humour broad
> He pleased the peasant, squire, and lord;
> Until grim death, with visage queer,
> Assumed Joe's trade of Auctioneer;
> Made him the Lot to practise on,
> With " going, going," and anon
> He knocked him down to " Poor Joe's gone ! "

Cork.

> Here lies Pat Steele, that's very true.
> Who was he ?   What was he ?
> What's that to you ?   He lies here
> Because he's dead; that's nothing new.

Melton Mowbray.

> This world's an Inn, and I her guest;
> I've eat and drank and took my rest
> With her awhile, and now I pay
> Her lavish bill and go my way.

St. Paul's, Mousehole, Cornwall.

> Old Doll Pentreath, one hundred age and two,
> Both born, and in Paul Parish buried too;
> Not in the Church 'mongst People great and high,
> But in the Churchyard doth old Dollie lie !

Awliscombe, Devon.

Here lie the remains of Jas. Pady, brickmaker, late of this parish. In hopes that his clay will be remoulded in a workmanlike manner far superior to his former perishable materials.

> Keep death and judgment always in your eye,
> Or else the devil off with you will fly,
> And in his kiln with brimstone ever fry.
> If you neglect the narrow road to seek
> You'll be rejected like a half-burnt brick.

Acton, Cornwall.

> Here lies entombed one Roger Morton,
> Whose sudden death was early brought on ;
> Trying one day his corn to mow off,
> The razor slipped, and cut his toe off ;
> The toe, or, rather, what it grew to,
> An inflammation quickly flew to ;
> The parts they took to mortifying,
> And poor dear Roger took to dying.

From very early days women have been the subject of satirical epitaphs by their relieved husbands, of which the best known is that wrongly ascribed to Dryden.

> Here lies my wife ; here let her lie :
> She's now at rest—and so am I !

Another version is :—

> Here lies my wife and Heaven knows
> Not less for mine than her repose.

At Old Greyfriars, Edinburgh, is the following :—

> Here snug in grave my wife doth lie !
> Now she's at rest, and so am I.

In Belfast.

> Beneath this stone lies Katherine, my wife,
> In death my comfort, and my plague through life.
> Oh, liberty !   But soft, I must not boast,
> She'll haunt me else, by jingo, with her ghost.
>
> *Patrick Leary.*

Other versions are :—

> Here rests my Spouse ; no pair through life
>   So *equal* liv'd as we did
> Alike we shar'd perpetual strife,
>   Nor knew I rest till she did.

> Here is my much lov'd Celia laid,
>   At rest from all her earthly labours !
> Glory to God ! peace to the dead !
>   And to the ears of all her neighbours.

> Beneath this stone and not above it
> Lie the remains of Anna Lovett ;
> Be pleased, dear reader, not to shove it,
> Lest she should come again above it.
> For 'twixt you and I, no one does covet
> To see again this Anna Lovett.

> Here lies the man Richard,
>   And Mary his wife ;
> Their surname was Pritchard,
>   They lived without strife ;
> And the reason was plain—
>   They abounded in riches,
> They had no care or pain,
>   And his wife wore the breeches.

AT ST. PATRICK'S, DUBLIN.

Underneath lies the body of Frederick, Duke of Schomberg, slain at the Battle of the Boyne, in the year 1690. The Dean and Chapter of this Church again and again besought the Heirs of the Duke to cause some monument to be here erected to his memory.

But when, after many entreaties by letters and by friends they found they could not obtain this Request, they themselves placed this stone; only that the indignant Reader may know where the ashes of Schomberg are deposited. Thus did the Fame only of his Virtue obtain more for him from strangers, than nearness of blood from his own Family.

This epitaph, as well as the three following, in the same cathedral, were written by Dean Swift and show that prelate's inclination to and powers of satire.

On Partridge, the Almanack Maker. Died 1708.
> Here, five feet deep, lies on his back
> A cobbler, starmonger and quack;
> Who, to the stars in pure good will,
> Does to his best look upward still.

> Weep, all you customers that use
> His pills, his almanacks, or shoes;
> And you that did your fortune seek,
> Step to his grave but once a week;
> This earth, which bears his body's print,
> You'll find has so much virtue in't,
> That I durst pawn my ears 'twill tell
> Whate'er concerns you full as well,
> In physick, stolen goods, or love,
> As he himself could, when above.

On John D'Amory, the Usurer. Died 1720.
> Beneath this verdant Hillock lies
> Demar the wealthy and the wise.
> His heirs, that he might safely rest,
> Have put his carcase in a chest.
> The very chest, in which, they say
> His *other self*, his money, lay.
> And if his heirs continue kind
> To that dear *self* he left behind,
> I dare believe that four in five
> Will think his better self alive.

On Judge Boat. Died 1723.

> Here lies Judge Boat within a coffin ;
> Pray, gentlefolks, forbear your scoffing.
> A Boat, a judge ! Yes ; where's the blunder ?
> A wooden judge is no such wonder.
> And in his robes you must agree,
> No boat was better deckt than he.
> 'Tis needless to describe him fuller ;
> In short, he was an able sculler.

MICKLEHURST.

> Life is an Inn, where all men bait,
> The waiter Time, the Landlord Fate ;
> Death is the score by all men due,
> I've paid my shot, and so must you.

CRAYFORD, KENT.
On a Parish Clerk.

To the memory of Peter Izod, who was 35 years parish clerk of this parish, and always proved himself a pious and mirthful man.

> The life of this clerk was just threescore and ten
> During half of which time he had sung out Amen.
> He married while young, like other young men ;
> His wife died one day, so he chanted Amen.
> A second he took, she departed—what then ?
> He married, and buried a third with Amen.
> Thus his joys and his sorrows were treble, but then
> His voice was deep bass, so he chanted Amen.
> On the horn he could blow as well as most men,
> But his horn was exalted in blowing Amen.
> He lost all his wind after three score and ten
> And here with three wives he waits till again,
> The trumpet shall rouse him to sing out Amen.

St. Giles', Cripplegate.

> Under this marble fair,
> Lies the body entomb'd of Gervase Aire ;
> He dy'd not of an ague fit,
> Nor surfeited by too much wit
> Methinks this was a wondrous death
> That *Aire* should die for want of breath.

Wood Ditton, near Newmarket.

On the gravestone is fixed an iron dish in accordance with the wishes of the deceased.

> Here lies my corpse, who was the man
> That loved a sop in the dripping pan ;
> But now believe me I am dead
> See here the pan stands at my head.
> Still for sops till the last I cried
> But could not eat, and so I died.
> My neighbours, they perhaps will laugh,
> When they do read my epitaph.
>
> 1753. *William Symons, aged* 80.

At Cross Kirk, Normavine, Shetland.

M.S.
Donald Robertson.
Born 1st of January, 1785, died 4th of June, 1848.
Aged 63 years.

He was a peaceable quiet man, and to all appearance a sincere Christian. His death was very much regretted, which was caused by the stupidity of Laurence Tulloch, of Clotherton, who sold him nitre instead of Epsom salts, by which he was killed in the space of 3 hours after taking a dose of it.

ANNANDALE.

On John Bell.

I Jocky Bell of Braikenbrow, lyes under this stane.
Five of my own sons laid it on my wame ;
I liv'd air my dayes, but sturt or strife
Was man o' my meat, and master o' my wife.
If you done better in your time, than I did in mine,
Take this stane aff my wame, and lay it on o' thine.

On John Adams, of Southwell, a carrier, who died of
drunkenness (the epitaph is by Byron).

John Adams lies here, of the parish of Southwell,
A carrier who carried his can to his mouth well ;
He carried so much, and he carried so fast,
He could carry no more—so was carried at last ;
For the liquor he drunk, being too much for one,
He could not carry-off—so he's now carri-on.

BEDDINGTON, SURREY.

Thomas Greenhill born and bredd in the famous
University of Oxon, Bachelor of Arts, and sometime
student of Magdalen Coll. Steward to the Noble
Knight, Sir Nic⁵ Carew, of Beddington, who deceased,
Sept. 17, 1624.

Under thy feet interr'd is here
A native born in Oxfordshire ;
First life and learning Oxford gave ;
Sarry him his death and grave !
He once a *Hill* was fresh and *Greene*
Now withered is not to be seene ;
Earth in earth shovell'd up is shut,
A *Hill* into a *Hole* is put ;
But darksome earth by Power Divine
Bright at last as the sun may shine.

ISLINGTON. 1805.

On Elizabeth Storer, aged 30.

> " . . . But that I am forbid
> To tell the secrets of my prison house,
> I could a tale unfold whose lightest word
> Would harrow up thy soul."

(The quotation is, of course, from Shakespeare.)

GLASGOW.

> Here lies Mass Andrew Gray,
> Of whom ne muckle good can I say!
> He was ne Quaker, for he had ne spirit ;
> He was ne Papist, for he had ne merit ;
> He was ne Turk, for he drank muckle wine ;
> He was ne Jew, for he eat muckle swine ;
> Full forty years he preached and le'ed
> For which God doomed him when he de'ed.

IN A DEVONSHIRE CHURCHYARD.

On the wife of Edward Greenwood, D.D.

> O Death, O Death, thou hast cut down
> The fairest *greenwood* in the town ;
> Her virtues and good qualities were such,
> She was worthy to marry a lord or a judge ;
> Yet such was her condescension and humility,
> She chose to marry me, a Doctor of Divinity
> For which heroic act she stands confess'd
> Above all women, the Phœnix of her sex ;
> And like that bird, one young she did beget,
> That she might not leave her friends disconsolate.
> My grief for her, alas ! is so sore,
> I can only write two lines more ;
> For this, and every other good woman's sake,
> Never lay a blister on a lying-in woman's back.

Wainfleet, Linc.

This epitaph on a monument erected in 1735 is one of the most pompous and ridiculous in existence.

Near this place
lye the remains
of Edward Barkham, Esq.
Who in his lifetime at his own expense
Erected the stately altar piece in this Church;
Furnished the Communion table
With a very rich crimson velvet carpet,
A cushion of the same, and a beautiful Common Prayer-book;
Likewise with two large flagons,
A chalice with a cover, together with a paten.
All of silver plate.
But above all (and what may very justly
preserve his name to latest posterity)
he gave and devised by will
To the curate of Wainfleet St. Marys and his
successors for ever
The sum of £35 per ann. (over and above his former salary)
With this clause, viz.
' provided the said curate and his successors
do and shall read prayers and preach
once every Sunday in the year for ever.'
So extraordinary an instance of securing
a veneration for the most awful part of our religion,
And so rare and uncommon a zeal
For promoting God's worship every Lord's day
(Divine Service being performed aforetime only every
other Sunday)
Forget not reader to proclaim to the world
that men in power and authority
Induced hereby to copy after so great an original,
May strive to excel each other
in doing likewise.

MISCELLANEOUS EPITAPHS

MISCELLANEOUS EPITAPHS

Epitaph by Dr. Lowth, late bishop of London, on a monument in the Church of Cuddesdon, Oxfordshire, to the memory of his daughter. Translated from the Latin.

Dear as thou didst in modest worth excel
More dear than in a daughter's name—farewell!
Farewell, dear Mary—but the hour is nigh
When, if I'm worthy, we shall meet on high :
Then shall I say, triumphant from the tomb,
"Come, to thy father's arms, dear Mary, come."

Frank Fry, of Christian Malford, Wilts, whose bones lie undisturbed in the churchyard of his native village, wrote for himself the following epitaph :—

Here lies I
Who did die
I lie did
As I die did
Old Frank Fry.

BROMLEY, KENT.

Sacred to the memory of Thomas Chase, Esq., formerly of this parish, born in the city of Lisbon the 1st of November 1729 ; and buried under the ruins of the same house where he first saw the light in the ever-memorable earthquake which befel that city the 1st of November 1755 : when after a most wonderful escape, he by degrees recovered from a very deplorable condition, and lived till the 20th of November, 1788, aged 59 years.

On Marian Wentworth.—T. Carew.

> And here the precious dust is laid,
> Whose purely-tempered clay was made
> So fine that it the guest betrayed—
> Else the soul grew so fast within,
> It broke the outward shell of sin,
> And so was hatched a Cherubin.

On an infant.—Coleridge.

> Ere sin could blight or sorrow fade,
> Death came with friendly care ;
> The opening Bud to Heaven conveyed
> And bade it blossom there.

On Hogarth.—Garrick.

> If genius fire thee, Reader, stay :
> If nature move thee, drop a tear :
> If neither touch thee, pass away.
> For Hogarth's honoured dust lies here.

On Hogarth.—Dr. Johnson.

> The hand of Art here torpid lies,
> That traced the essential form of Grace.
> Here death has closed the attentive eyes
> That saw the manners in the face.

Mrs. Hemans—on her tomb at Dublin.

> Calm on the bosom of thy God,
> Fair spirit, rest thee now :
> Even while with us thy footstep trod,
> His seal was on thy brow.

> Dust ! to its narrow house beneath !
>   Soul ! to its place on high !
> They that have seen thy look in death
>   No more may fear to die.

On Quin the Actor.—Garrick.

> The scene is changed, I am no more :
> Death's the last act—now all is o'er.

Ben Jonson.

> Underneath this stone doth lie
> As much beauty as could die ;
> Which in life did harbour give
> To more virtue than doth live.

Southey.—W. S. Landor.

> Few tears, nor these too warm, are shed
> By poet over poet dead.
> Without premeditated lay
> To catch the crowd, I only say,
> As over Southey's tomb I bend,—
> The best of mortals was my friend.

On an infant.—Robert Lowth, D.D.

> Just to her lips the cup of life she pressed,
> Found the taste bitter, and refused the rest ;
> She felt averse to life's returning day
> And slowly sighed her little soul away.

On Henry Martin, died in Persia, 1812.—Macaulay.

> For that dear Name,
> Through every form of danger, death and shame,
> Onward he journeyed to a happier shore,
> Where danger, death and shame assault no more.

On Sir T. Gravener.—Sir T. Wyatt.

> Under this stone here lieth at rest
> A friendly man, a worthy knight ;
> Whose heart and mind was ever prest
> To favour truth, to further right.

IN BROMLEY CHURCH.

Near this place lies the body of
Elizabeth Monk
who departed this life
on the 27th day of August, 1753
Aged 101.
She was the widow of John Monk late of this
Parish, Blacksmith,
Her second husband
to whom she had been a wife near fifty years
by whom she had no children :
And of the issue of the first marriage none lived
to the second
But Virtue
would not suffer her to be childless
An infant, to whom and to whose Father
and Mother she had been nurse
(such is the uncertainty of temporal prosperity)
became dependent upon strangers
for the necessaries of life
To him she afforded the protection of a Mother
This parental charity
was returned with filial affection :
and she was supported, in the feebleness of age
by him whom she had cherished in
the helplessness of Infancy.

To preserve the memory of this person : and yet
more, to perpetuate the lesson of her life, this stone was
erected by voluntary contribution.

According to the Everyday Book, which gives considerable
confirmatory evidence, there was born in 1500 in Bolton
near Catterick and Richmond, in Yorkshire, a man who
lived to be one hundred and sixty-nine years of age, named
Henry Jenkins. He died in the neighbouring village of
Ellerton-under-Swale, but was buried in Bolton Churchyard where a small pillar was erected to his memory and this

epitaph composed by Dr. Thomas Chapman, Master of Magdalene College, Cambridge, from 1746 to 1760, engraved upon a monument in Bolton Church.

Blush not, Marble !
To rescue from oblivion
the memory of
Henry Jenkins
a person obscure in birth
But of a life truly memorable :
for
He was enriched
With the goods of Nature
If not of Fortune :
and happy
In the duration
if not variety
of his enjoyments :
And, tho' the partial world
Despised and disregarded
His low and humble state
The equal eye of Providence
Beheld and blessed it,
With a patriarch's health, and length of days :
To teach mistaken man
these blessings
Were intail'd on temperance
A life of labour, and a mind at ease.
He lived to the amazing age of
169
Was here interred December 6th
1670
And had this justice done to his memory
1743.

BUDOCH CHURCHYARD, AND OTHER PLACES.

" Who gathered this flower ? " The gardener answered,
" The Master." And his fellow-servant held his peace.

SUTTON.

> This monument presents unto your view
> A woman rare, in whom all grace divine
> Faith, Love, Zeal, Piety, in splendid hue
> With sacred knowledge perfectly did shine.
> Since, then, example teach, learn you by this
> To mount the steppes of everlasting bliss.

In the Churchyard of St. Lawrence at York is a tablet commemorating the death by drowning in the Ouse, August 1830, of six young persons, brothers and sisters, with the following inscription.

> Mark the brief story of a Summer's day !
> At noon, youth, health, and beauty launched away :
> Ere eve, Death wreck'd the bark, and quenched that light ;
> Their parents' home was desolate at night ;
> Each pass'd alone that gulph no eye can see,
> They met, next moment, in eternity.
> Friend, kinsman, stranger, dost thou ask me where ?
> Seek God's right hand, and hope to find them there.

THE PRESBYTERIAN CEMETERY, BRIGHTON.
> > Four infant sons of George Sawyer,
> > 1847-50.

> Bold Infidelity ! turn pale and die ;
> Near to this stone 4 infants' ashes lie.
> Say, are they lost or saved ?
> If death's by sin, they sinned because they're here,
> If Heaven's by works, in Heaven they can't appear ;
> Reason, ah, how depraved !
> Revere the page, the knot's untied ;
> They died, for Adam sinned.
> They live, for Jesus died.

From Norwich Cemetery, a testimonial the modern housewife will read with envy :

Hannah Weeds,
Died August 1880,
Aged 70.

For upwards of thirty-five years housekeeper to Mr. and Mrs. ——. A God-fearing woman, who knew what Christian service meant. Regarded rather as a friend than as a domestic. She remarkably displayed throughout punctuality, economy, order, industry, integrity, and treated the interests of master and mistress as her own.

Was always trusted and trustworthy.
Well done, good and faithful servant.
This stone is erected by their son.

On Hobson, the celebrated Cambridge carrier, the original of " Hobson's Choice," Milton wrote two humorous epitaphs, one of which is as follows.

Rest, that gives all men life, gave him his death,
And too much breathing put him out of breath ;
Nor were it contradiction to affirm
Too long vacation hastened on his term.
Thereby to drive the time away he sickened,
Fainted, and died, nor would with all be quickened.
Ease was his chief disease ; and, to judge right
He died for weariness that his cart went light :
His leisure told him that his time was come
And lack of load made his life burdensome :
Obedient to the Moon, he spent his date
In course reciprocal, and had his fate
Linked to the mutual flowing of the seas :
His letters are delivered all and gone
Only remains this superscription.

GREEN BAY, JAMAICA.

Here lies the body of L. Galdy, Esquire, who departed this life at Port Royal on the 22nd December 1739. Aged 80. He was born at Montpelier in France, but he left that Country for his Religion, and came to settle in this Island, when he was swallowed up in the Great Earthquake in the year 1692, and by the Providence of God was by another shock thrown into the Sea and miraculously saved by swimming until a boat took him up. He lived many years after in great reputation beloved by all that knew him, and much lamented at his death.

The following is by Ben Jonson on Labathiel Pavy, a boy who died in his thirteenth year, a " prodigy " actor of the parts of old men.

> Weep with me all you that read
>   This little story,
> And know for whom a tear you shed
>   Death's self is sorry.
>
> 'Twas a child that did so thrive
>   In grace and feature,
> That heaven and nature seemed to strive
>   Which owned the creature.
>
> Years he numbered, scarce thirteen
>   When fates turned cruel,
> Yet three-fill'd Zodiacs had he been
>   The stage's jewel.
>
> And did act, what now we moan
>   Old men so duly,
> As sooth, the Parcie thought him one
>   He played so truly.

An epitaph on a tablet near the west door of Lincoln Cathedral.

Here is Entombed

Dame Harriot daughter of Lieut : General Churchill :
wife in her first marriage to Sr. Everard Fawkener, Kt.
in her second to Governour Pownall.

She dyed Feb. 6 : 1777 aged 51.

Her person was that of animated animating beauty,
with a complexion of the most exquisite brilliancy
unfaded when she fell.

Her understanding was of such quickness and reach of thought
that her knowledge, although she had learning,
was instant, and original.

Her heart warmed with universal benevolence
to the highest degree of sensibility,
had a ready tear for pity :
and glowed with friendship as with a sacred and inviolate fire
her love to those who were blest to it,
was happiness.

Her sentiments were correct, refined, elevated ;
her manners so cheerful and winning—amiable.
That while she was admired she was beloved ;
and while she enlightened and enliven'd :
she was the delight of the world in which she lived.

She was formed for life.

She was prepared for death ;
which being
" A Gentle Wafting to Immortality,"
She lives
where life is real.

An epitaph on a gallant general killed in South Africa.

No longer now in Scotland's castles old,
    Thy voice is heard—The country mourns thy loss.
The " Roll of Honour " bears thy name in gold,
    While thou art sleeping 'neath the Southern Cross.

A quaint epitaph to Mrs. Mary Kendall in Westminster Abbey.

Those admirable qualities.
In which she was equalled by few of her sex, surpassed by none,
Rendered her every way worthy of that close union and friendship,
In which she lived with
The Lady Catherine Jones.

Mrs. Cyril Martineau.

Underneath this stone does lie,
As much beauty as can die,
Which in life did harbour give
To more goodness than could live.

Epitaph in Almondsbury Church, Gloucester.

Of all the creatures God has made, there is none so miserable as man.

For all dumb creatures, have no misfortune do befall them, but what come by nature. But man, thro' his own folly and against his own inclination, brings himself into 1,000 griefs both of soul and body, as for example—

Our father had two children, and against his knowledge he committed the sin of Idolatry upon them.

For had our father done his duty towards God I part in 1,000 as he did towards us, when he prayed God to spare our lives God might have heard his prayer. But God is a jealous God for punishing the faults of parents upon the children.

Tho' the sins of our father have deprived us of the light of the sun, thanks be to God, we enjoy more great, more sweet, more blessed Light, which is the presence of God the maker of all lights to whom be honour and glory!

ELVET CHURCHYARD, DURHAM.

On John Bolton—an artist.

Ingenious artist ! few thy skill surpast
In works of art. Yet death hath beat at last.
Tho' conquered. Yet thy deeds will ever shine
Time cant destroy a genius large as thine.

Richard Brandon, the official executioner of the City of
London, and the man who is supposed to have decapitated
Charles the First.

Who do you think lies buried here ?
One that did help to make hemp dear.
The poorest subject did abhor him
And yet his King did kneel before him ;
He would his master not betray,
Yet he his master did destroy
And yet as Judas—in records to be found
Judas had thirty pence—he thirty pound.

Lines on the grave of Jackson—Pugilist.
In the West London Cemetery.

" Stay, traveller," the Roman second said,
To mark the classic dust beneath it laid :
" Stay, traveller," this brief memorial cries,
And read the moral with attentive eyes.
Hast thou a lion's heart, a giant's strength,
Exult not, for these gifts must yield at length ;
Do health and symmetry adorn thy frame,
The mouldering bones below possessed the same ;
Does love, does friendship, every step attend,
This man ne'er made a foe, nor lost a friend :
But death full soon dissolves all human ties,
And, his last combat o'er here Jackson lies.

The following was inscribed in Peterborough Cathedral
to the memory of Sir Richard Worme.

Does worm eat Worme ? Knight Worme this truth
　　confirms :
For here, with worms, lies Worme, a dish for worms.
Does Worme eat worm ? Sure Worme will this deny,
For worms with Worme, a dish for Worme don't lie.
'Tis so, and 'tis not so, for free from worms
'Tis certain Worme is blessed without his worms.

1589.

On a smuggler who was shot while endeavouring to evade
arrest. PATCHAM, SUSSEX.

Sacred to the Memory of
Daniel Scales
Who was unfortunately shot on Tuesday evening
Nov. 7, 1796.
Alas, swift flew the fatal lead,
Which pierced through this young man's head.
He instant fell, resigned his breath,
And closed his languid eyes in death.
And you to whom this languid stone draw near
Oh ! pray let fall the pitying tear.
From this sad instance may we all
Prepare to meet Jehovah's call.

Epitaph on a Gardener.

Beneath this sod an honest gardener's laid,
Who long was thought the tulip of his trade ;
A life of many years to him was known,
But now he's withered like a rose oerblown.
Like a transplanted flower be this his doom,
Fading in this world, in the next to bloom.

Quoted in the Year Book 1832.

Epsom.

> Here lieth the carcase
> Of honest Charles Parkhurst,
> Who ne'er could dance or sing
> But always was true to
> His Sovereign Lord the King,
> Charles the First.

> > *Died Dec.* 20.   1704.   *Aged 96.*

Sutton.

On a Butcher.

> A steady friend to youth, a heart sincere,
> In dealing strictly just, in conscious clear,
> Here Boorer lies,—Oh stone record his name,
> Virtues like these may others boast the same,
> When pitying sorrow drops a tender tear,
> The last sad tribute to a friend sincere.

This is a literal copy of a somewhat ambiguous tombstone at Ivy Churchyard in Kent.

> In memory of
> Hannah Margaret
> Daughter of Matthew and Hannah B.
> who died Nov. 27, 1827, aged 5 years.

> > Great his our grief
> > Great was her pain,
> > Great his our loss
> > Great his her gain
> > And near this place lie the remains
> > of two of their infants.

In Sevenoaks Churchyard is the following :—

> Grim death took me without any warning,
> I was well at night, and dead at nine in the morning.

Goldsmith's epitaph on Sir Joshua Reynolds.

Here Reynolds is laid, and, to tell you my mind,
He has not left a wiser or better behind ;
His pencil was striking, resistless and grand ;
His manners were gentle, complying, and bland.
Still born to improve us in every part,
His pencil our faces—his manners our heart :
To coxcombs averse, yet most civilly steering :
When they judged without skill, he was still hard of hearing :
When they talked of their Raphaels, Correggios and stuff,
He shifted his trumpet and only took snuff.

HYTHE.   On a fisherman.

      His net old fisher George long drew
        Shoals upon shoal he caught,
      Till Death came hauling for his due,
        And made poor George his draught.
      Death fishes on through various shapes ;
      In vain it is to fret ;
      No fish or fisherman escapes
      Death's all enclosing net.

Epitaphs to old servants have generally the virtue of sincerity, and for a record of faithful service it would be difficult to beat one in Disley churchyard :

" Here lyeth interred the body of Joseph Watson, buried June 3rd, 1733, aged 104 years. He was park keeper at Lyne more than 64 years, and was the first that perfected the art of driving the stags."

Watson, according to a Chester historian, " was in his 103rd year at the hunting and killing of a buck with the Hon. George Warren, in his park at Poynton, he being the fifth generation of the Warren family he had performed that diversion with in Poynton Park."

HIGHDOWN HILL.

In the tomb of a miller is a rough sculpture of Death running away from Time who pursues. Death, a skeleton, holds a spear and Time a glass. Beneath is the following inscription :—

> Death, why so fast ?—pray stop your hand,
> And let my glass run out its sand :
> As neither Death nor Time will stay,
> Let us implore the present day,
> Why start you at the skeleton ?
> 'Tis your picture which you shun ;
> Alive it did resemble thee,
> And thou, other dead, like that shall be :
> But tho' Death must have his will
> Yet old Time prolongs the date,
> Till the measure we shall fill,
> That's allotted us by Fate !—
> When that's done, then Time and Death
> Both agree to take our breath.

CALSTOCK, CORNWALL.

> 'Twas by a fall I caught my death :
> No man can tell his time or breath.
> I might have died as soon as then
> If I had had physician men.

On Abraham Newland, Chief Cashier of the Bank of England, died 1807.

> Beneath this stone old Abr'am lies :
> Nobody laughs and nobody cries :
> Where he's gone or how he fares,
> Nobody knows and no one cares.

The following were copied from Indian tombstones.

In memory of Sergeant H. Orchard, 8th (The King's) Regiment, who died at Murree, Punjab, in 1876, aged 26 years.

> Farewell, dear comrades, one and all, good-bye,
> My stay was short but God knows why
> He called me to Himself—He knew but why—
> From the King's Regt.   I hope I was prepared to die.

In memory of the wife of Conductor Ross, who died in 1826 at Agra.   She had been blind for 14 years.

> Was ever anything e'er so Rare,
> E'en life itself half so dear
> To mortal being in this Orb of Light,
> As those blessed members the eye's sight.

In memory of Br. Major Eagle, 3rd Regt. N. I., who died in 1811, at Delhi.   Monument erected by his widow.

> Silent grave, to thee I trust
> This precious pile of worthy dust,
> Keep it safe in the sacred tomb,
> Until a wife shall ask for room.

East Dereham.

> Yet who with warmth the public triumph feel
> Of talents, dignified by sacred zeal,
> Here, to devotion's band devoutly just,
> Pay your fond tribute due to Cowper's dust.
> England, exulting in his spotless fame,
> Ranks with her dearest sons his favourite name.
> Sense, fancy, wit, suffice not all to raise
> So clear a title to affection's praise.
> His highest honours to the heart belong ;
> His virtues formed the magic of his song.
>
> *Hayley.*
>
> 1800. *William Cowper.* *Aged* 69.

An epitaph in Highworth Churchyard on an aged gipsy woman, said to have been the original of Scott's " Meg Merrilies."

" Being dead yet speaketh."

Beneath lies one—they say could tell
By the magic of her spell,
By the most unerring signs,
By the hand's mysterious signs,
What our earthly lot should be,
What our future destiny.
But the dust that lies below
Speaks more truly, for e'en now,
It bids the proud, ere life is past,
Contemplate their lot at last,
When this world's gaudy vision's gone,
When high and low shall be as one,
When rich and poor, and vile and just,
Shall mingle in one common dust.

Aug. 5th, 1830.

The most extraordinary attempt at advertising which is known to exist is to be found at the Churchyard at Godalming, Surrey, where the following epitaph was placed upon a tombstone.

Sacred
to the Memory of
Nathaniel Godbold, Esq.
Inventor and Proprietor
of that excellent medicine
The Vegetable Balsam
for the cure of Consumptions and Asthmas.
He departed this life
The 17th day of December 1799
Aged 69 years
Hic cineres, ubique Fama.

At the Church of St. John, Clerkenwell, is a stone in memory of the late Mrs. Sarah Newman, of No. 63, Cowcross Street, St. Sepulchre, and is interesting as an amplification of the ever-recurring epitaph " Affliction sore," &c. She is made to say :

> Pain was my portion,
> Physic was my food
> Groans was my devotion,
> Drugs did me no good.
> Christ was my physician
> Knew what way was best,
> To ease me of my pain,
> He took my soul to rest.

> Here lies
> Captain Ernest Bloomfield
> accidentally shot by his orderly
> March 2nd 1789.
> " Well done, good and faithful servant."

EDMONTON.

To the Memory of Charles Lamb.
Died 1834, aged 59.

Farewell, dear Friend ! That smile, that harmless mirth,
No more shall gladden our domestic hearth ;
That rising tear, with pain forbid to flow,
Better than words, no more assuage our woe ;
That hand, outstretched from small but well-earned store,
Yield succour to the destitute no more.
Yet thou art not all lost ; through many an age
With sterling sense and humour shall thy page
Win many an English bosom, pleas'd to see
That old and happier vein revived in thee.
This for our earth ! and if with friends we share
Our joys in heaven, we hope to meet thee there.

H. F. Cary.

The following epitaph is placed over the grave of a railway
engineer in Bromsgrove Churchyard.

My engine now is cold and still,
No water does my boiler fill :
My coke affords its flame no more ;
My days of usefulness are o'er ;
My wheels deny their noted speed—
No more my guiding hand they need :
My whistle, too, has lost its tone—
Its shrill and thrilling sounds are gone ;
My valves are now thrown open wide ;
My flanges all refuse to guide ;
My clacks, also though once so strong,
Refuse to aid the busy throng ;
No more I feel each urging breath—
My steam is now condensed in death
Life's railway's o'er, each station's past ;
In death I'm stopp'd, and rest at last.
Farewell, dear friends, and cease to weep ;
In Christ I'm safe—in Him I sleep.

GRASMERE.

Blest be the Church, that watching o'er the needs
Of infancy, provides a timely shower,
Whose virtue changes to a Christian flower,
A growth from sinful nature's bed of weeds !
Fittest beneath the sacred roof proceeds
The ministration ; while parental love
Looks on, and grace descendeth from above.
As the high service pledges now, now pleads,
Should vain thoughts outspread their wings and fly,
To meet the coming hours of festal mirth,
The tombs which hear and answer that brief cry,
The infant's notice of his second birth,
Recall the wandering soul to sympathy
With what man hopes from Heaven, yet fears from earth.

1850. *William Wordsworth*. *Aged* 80.

P

From Newbridge Churchyard in Ireland :

In memory of Trumpet Major Keeling, 8th Hussars, killed by a fall from his horse.

Of Nature's chain one link lies buried here,
A soldier truthful, honest, and sincere,
By many known, by all beloved was he,
His maxims true, his maxim honesty.
In prime of life death stopped his bright career,
To-day in health, to-morrow on his bier.
Then rest ye, Keeling, rest, nor fear the route,
Till the last trumpet sounds the great " Turn-out."

Sacred to the memory of Robert Southey whose mortal remains are interred in the adjoining churchyard.

He was born at Bristol
August XII, MDCCLXXIV.
and died, after a residence of nearly XL years, at
Greta Hall, in this Parish, March XXI, MDCCCXLIII.
This monument was erected by friends of Robert Southey.

Ye hills and vales, whose beauty hither drew
The poet's steps, and fixed him here, on you
His eyes have closed ! And ye, loved books, no more
Shall Southey feed upon your precious lore.
To works that ne'er shall forfeit their renown,
Adding immortal labours of his own.
Whether he traced historic truth with zeal,
For the State's guidance or the Church's weal,
Or Fancy, disciplined by studious art
Informed his pen, or wisdom of the heart,
Or judgments sanctioned in the patriot's mind
By reverence for the rights of all mankind.
Wide were his aims, yet in no human breast
Could private feelings find a holier nest.
His joys, his griefs, have vanished as a cloud
From Skiddaw's top, but he to heaven was vowed.

Wordsworth.

In Canongate Churchyard, Edinburgh.

To the Memory of
Robert Burns, the Ayrshire Bard ;
who was born at Doonside
On the 29th of January 1759,
and died at Dumfries
On the 22nd of July 1796

O Rabbie Burns, the Man, the Brither,
And art thou gone—and gone for ever ;
And hast thou crossed that unknown river,
          Life's dreary bound ?
Like thee, where shall we find anither
          The world around ?
Go to your sculptur'd tombs, ye Great,
In a' the tinsel trash of state ;
But by thy honest turf, I'll wait,
          Thou man of Worth,
And weep the sweetest poet's fate,
          E'er lived on earth.

Here lies
Robert Fergusson, Poet.
Born 5th Sept. 1751—Died Oct. 16, 1774.

No sculptured Marble here, nor pompous lay,
No storied urn, nor animated Bust ;
This simple stone directs pale Scotia's way
To pour her sorrows o'er her Poet's dust.

Campton, Bedford.

Here lie the remains of Robert Bloomfield.
He was born at Honington, in Suffolk, Dec. 3, 1766 ;
and died at Shefford, Aug. 19, 1823.
Let his wild native wood-notes tell the rest.

Wᴇsᴛ Wʏᴄᴏᴍʙᴇ.

> Here lies a man misfortune could not bend,
> Praised as a poet, honour'd as a friend ;
> Tho' his youth kindled with the love of fame,
> Within his bosom glow'd a brighter flame !
> Whene'er his friends with sharp affliction bled,
> And from the wounded deer the herd was fled,
> *Whitehead* stood forth, the healing balm applied,
> Nor quitted their distresses—'till he died.

Garrick.

1774.   *Paul Whitehead, aged* 64.

Elizabeth Inchbald, died 1821, aged 69.

> Lo ! the white tablet, emblem of the mind
> Of infant purity, below enshrin'd,
> Marked by the tribute of parental sighs—
> Here too at rest lamented Inchbald lies.
> The child presag'd, in time's maturing hour,
> To rise a beauteous intellectual flower !
> Yet, ah ! While Hope indulged a fond delight,
> The cherished blossom felt Death's fatal blight !
> Thus Inchbald's youth presag'd a future claim
> To moral dignity and mental fame,
> But Time, what nature form'd with powers so rare,
> Touch'd with prophetic zeal, was proud to spare ;
> Proud to prolong her useful mortal state,
> E'en to the verge of our allotted date,
> To spread the works of her creative mind,
> That while amusing, meliorate mankind.
> Her life was just, benevolent and sage,
> As truth proclaims in her instructive page !
> Religion consecrates her honour'd bier,
> And a true Christian waits for mercy here.

J. Taylor.

James Beattie, died 1803. Aged 68.
(Written by himself.)

Escaped the gloom of mortal life, a soul
 Here leaves his mouldering tenement of clay,
Safe, where no cares their whelming billows roll,
 No doubts bewilder, and no hopes betray.

Like thee, I once have stemm'd the sea of life ;
 Like thee, have languish'd after heavy joys ;
Like thee, have laboured in the stormy strife ;
 Been grieved for trifles and amused with toys !

Yet for awhile 'gainst Passion's threatful blast
 Let steady Reason urge the struggling oar ;
Shot through the dreary gloom, the morn at last
 Gives to thy longing eye the blissful shore.

Forget my frailties, thou art also frail ;
 Forgive my lapses, for thyself mayst fall :
Nor read unmoved my artless tender tale,
 I was a friend, O man ! to thee, to all.

IN BERKSHIRE.

This modest stone, what few vain marbles can
May truly say, here lies an *honest man* :
A poet bless'd beyond the poet's fate,
Whom heaven kept sacred from the proud and great ;
Foe to loud praise, and friend to learned ease,
Content with science on the vale of peace !
Calmly he looked on *either* life ; and here
Saw nothing to regret, nor there to fear ;
From Nature's temperate feast rose satisfied ;
He lived respected, and lamented died.

Pope.

1730. *Elijah Fenton. Aged* 47.

Pope also wrote one on John Gay, whose own epitaph is in Westminster Abbey.

> Of manners gentle, of affection mild,
> In wit a man, simplicity a child ;
> With native humour, temp'ring virtuous rage,
> Form'd to delight at once, and lash the age ;
> Above temptation in a low estate,
> And incorrupted, e'en among the great ;
> A safe companion, and an easy friend,
> Unblam'd through life, lamented in thy end ;
> These are thy honours ! not that here thy bust
> Is mixt with heroes, or with King's thy dust ;
> But that the worthy and the good shall say
> Striking their pensive bosoms—Here lies Gay.

ALL SAINTS', CAMBRIDGE.

> Warm with fond hope, and learning's sacred flame,
> To Granta's bowers this youthful Poet came ;
> Unconquer'd powers, th' immortal mind displayed,
> But worn with anxious thought the frame decay'd,
> Pale o'er his lamp, and in his cell retir'd,
> The Martyr student faded and expir'd.
> Of Genius, Taste and Piety sincere,
> Too early lost, 'midst duties too severe ;
> Foremost to mourn was generous Southey seen.
> He told the tale, and show'd what White *had been*,
> Nor told in vain, for o'er the Atlantic wave,
> A Wanderer came and sought the Poet's grave,
> On yon low stone he saw his lonely name
> And raised this fond memorial to his fame.

W. Smyth.
1806. *Henry Kirke White. Aged* 21.

FELPHAM.

William Hayley, died 1820, aged 75.

> Hayley ! beloved friend ! though round thy head
> The Muses' wreath its graceful foliage spread ;

Though Fame was long thy talent's rich reward,
And Fashion smiled upon Serena's bard;
Though thou wast formed in polished courts to shine,
And Learning's stores and playful wit was thine;
Though Cowper's self thy tuneful strains approved!
And praised the poet while the man he loved;
Cowper, who lives in thy recording page,
To interest, charm, and teach the future age;
Oh, not on these alone thy honours rest,
But that thy name pale Want and Misery blest!
That such thy glowing zeal for all mankind,
So vast thy charity, so unconfined,
Thy hand had spread a scene of blessing round,
If ample wealth thy ardent hopes had crowned,
That whatsoe'er thy bounty could impart
Was given to teach the mind and cheer the heart;
Neglected Talent's drooping head to raise,
And lead young Genius on by generous praise.
Yet, Bard beloved! this higher meed be thine,
Faith in thy Saviour cheered thy life's decline;
Nor by that God on whom thy hopes relied,
Was the sweet recompense of faith denied.
He gave thee strength to smile 'midst torturing pain,
And even the slightest murmur still restrain;
He cheered with pious hope thy dying bed,
He on thy soul the Christian's sunshine shed;
And crowned, to prove his favour's best increase,
A life of kindness with a death of peace.

Mrs. Opie.

TROWBRIDGE.

Sacred
To the Memory of
The Rev. G. Crabbe, L.L.B.
Who died on the 3rd of Feb. 1832, in the 78th year of his age
And the 18th of his services as Rector of this Parish.
Born in humble life he made himself what he was;
Breaking through the obscurity of his birth by the
force of his Genius;

Yet he never ceased to feel for the less fortunate; entering, as his works testify, into the sorrows and wants of the Poorest of his Parishioners, and so discharging the duties of a Pastor and a Magistrate as to endear himself to all around him. As a writer, he cannot better be described than in the words of a great poet, his contemporary

"‧Tho' nature's sternest painter, yet her best."

This monument was erected by some of his affectionate friends and Parishioners.

HIGHGATE.

Stop, Christian passer-by ; stop, child of God,
And read with gentle breast. Beneath this sod
A poet lies, or that which once seemed he !
O ! lift a prayer in thought for S. T. C. !
That he who many a year with toil of breath,
Found death in life—may here find life in death !
Mercy for praise, to be forgiven, for fame !
He asked, and hoped through Christ. Do thou the same.

1834. *Samuel Taylor Coleridge. Aged* 61.
(Written by himself.)

CHICHESTER.

Ye, who the merits of the dead revere,
Who hold misfortune sacred, genius dear,
Regard this tomb, where Collins' hapless name
Solicits kindness with a double claim.
Tho' nature gave him, and tho' science taught
The fire of fancy, and the reach of thought,
Severely doomed to penury's extreme,
He passed in madd'ning pain, life's feverish dream,
While rays of genius only serv'd to show,
The thickening horror, and exalt his woe
Ye walls, that echoed to his frantic moan,

Guard the due records of this grateful stone ;
Strangers to him, enamour'd of his lays,
This fond memorial to his talents raise :
For this the ashes of a Bard require,
Who touched the tend'rest notes of pity's lyre ;
Who joined pure faith to strong poetic powers :
Who, in reviving reason's lucid hours,
Sought on one book his troubled mind to rest,
And rightly deemed the Book of God the best.

Hayley.
1756. *William Collins. Aged* 36.

BUNHILL FIELDS.

To real merit due, this humble song,
Watts (now no more) to thee be sacred long.
Sweet were thy numbers, as thy soul was great ;
In virtue rich, with piety replete :
In vain to thee vice sounds her soft alarms,
In vain she spreads her gay alluring charms :
The steady zeal, the wily foe o'erthrow,
And gave her veil'd deformity to view.
From thee our youths enlarged their op'ning views,
Learned heavenly truths, and reason's proper use ;
With vary'd beauties grac'd thy tuneful lyre,
To charm, deter, correct, improve, inspire ;
From tort'ring fears the soul depressed to free,
E'en David's strains receiv'd new charms from thee.
In haste to aid, but in resentment slow,
An ardent friend, and quick-forgiving foe :
Oh ! may thy soul, now loos'd from mortal clay,
Wing its swift flight to realms of endless day ;
There all its glories, all its joys improve,
In scenes of perfect purity and love.

1748. *Isaac Watts, D.D. Aged* 74.

KENTISBEARE, DEVON.

> To youth, to age, alike, this Tablet pale
> Tells the brief moral of its tragic tale.
> Art thou a parent ? Reverence this bier,
> The parent's fondest hopes lie buried here,
> Art thou a youth, prepared in life to start,
> With opening talents and a generous heart,
> Fair hopes and flattering prospects all thine own ?
> Lo ! here their end—a monumental stone.
> But let submission tame each sorrowing thought,
> Heaven crown'd its champion ere the fight was fought.
>
> *Sir W. Scott.*
> 1830. *Rev. George Scott.*

TWICKENHAM.

> Died 1744.
> Alexander Pope.
> For one who would not be buried in Westminster Abbey.

> Heroes and Kings your distance keep,
> In peace let one poor poet sleep,
> Who never flattered folks like you,
> Let Horace blush and Virgil too.

Besides the above, placed by Bishop Warburton to his memory, Pope wrote another for himself as follows :

> Under this marble, or under this sill,
> Or under this turf, or e'en what they will ;
> Whatever an heir, or a friend in his stead,
> Or any good creature shall lay o'er my head,
> Lies one who ne'er cared, and still cares not a pin
> What they said, or may say, of the mortal within !
> But, who, living and dying, serene, still and free,
> Trusts in God, that as well as he was, he shall be.

GOSNEVIN, IRELAND.

> Read Tickell's name, and gently tread the clay
> Where lie his sole Remains that could decay !
> Then pensive sigh, and through fair Science trace,

His mind adorn'd with every pleasing Grace.
Worth such as Rome would have confessed her own ;
Wit, such as Athens would have proudly shown.
Substance to thought, and weight to fancy joined ;
A judgment perfect, and a Taste refined.
Admired by Gay, by Addison beloved ;
Esteemed by Swift, by Pope himself approv'd ;
His spirit, rais'd by that Sublime he knew,
Hence to the seat of bright Perfection flew,
Leaving, to sorrowful Clotilda here,
A mournful Heart, and never-ceasing tear.

Clancy.

1740. *Thomas Tickell.* *Aged* 54.

Died 1743. Aged 46.

Richard Savage.
Whom Phœbus favour'd, on whom favour frowned,
Lies deep, beneath this consecrated ground ;
Savage the name—he was designed by fate,
That err'd at his conception, to be great.
And such he was, in boundless wit and pride,
Title and heir his mother's lust denied.
His life was want, yet could his duteous verse,
The cruel's praise, that help withheld, rehearse
Danger extreme, th' unhappy lawless knew,
And woes he felt, as woes were all his due ;
Twice sovereign mercy found a queen to save,
From pitying Heaven, to end his cares—a grave.

St. Giles', Cripplegate.
To the memory of
John Milton
Author of Paradise Lost.
Born December 1608, died November 1674.
His father John Milton, died March 1646.
They were both interred in this Church.

In addition to the memorial to Thomas Gray, the poet, a monument stands in a field adjoining the churchyard of Stoke Poges, consisting of a large stone sarcophagus, supported on a square pedestal, on the sides of which is the following inscription and extracts from his Ode to Eton College and the Elegy written in a Country Churchyard.

This monument in honour of
Thomas Gray
Was erected A.D 1799.
Among the scenery
Celebrated by that great Lyric and Elegiac Poet.
He died in 1771
And lies unnoticed in the adjoining churchyard ;
Under the tombstone
On which he piously and pathetically
Recorded the interment
Of his Aunt and lamented Mother.

LICHFIELD CATHEDRAL.

Amid these aisles, where once his precepts showed
The Heavenward pathway which in life he trode,
This simple tablet marks a Father's bier ;
And those he lov'd in life in death are near,
For him, for them, a daughter bade it rise
Memorial of domestic charities.
Still would you know why o'er the marble spread
In female grace the willow droops her head ;
Why on her branches, silent and unstrung,
The minstrel harp, is emblematic hung,
What Poet's voice is smothered here in dust
Till waked to join the chorus of the just,
Lo ! one brief line an answer sad supplies,
Honour'd, belov'd, and mourn'd here Seward lies.
Her worth, her warmth of heart, our sorrows say,—
Go seek her genius in her living lay.

Sir W. Scott.

HALESOWEN, SALOP.

Whoe'er thou art, with reverence tread
These sacred mansions of the dead !
Not that the monumental bust,
Or sumptuous tomb here guards the dust.
Of rich or great, let wealth, rank, birth,
Sleep undistinguished in the earth ;
This simple urn records a name,
Which shines with more exalted fame.
Reader ! if genius, taste refined,
Of native elegance of mind ;
If virtue, science, manly sense,
If wit that never gave offence,
The clearest head, the tenderest heart,
In thy esteem e'er claimed a part,
Ah ! smite thy breast, and drop a tear,
For know thy Shenstone's dust lies here.

1763. William Shenstone. Aged 49.

WALLASEY.

Led by Religion's bright and cheering ray,
He taught the way to Heaven, and went that way ;
And while he held the Christian life to view,
He was himself the Christian that he drew.

1814. Rev. George Briggs. Aged 85.

PETERBOROUGH CATHEDRAL.

Spencer Madan, D.D.
Lord Bishop of Peterborough
Translated from the See of Bristol in 1794
Died November the 8th, 1813.
In the 85th year of his age,
In Sacred sleep the pious Bishop lies,
Say not in Death—a good Man never dies.

MISERRIMUS.

In the north aisle of the Cloister of Worcester Cathedral is a sepulchral slab, which bears only the word Miserrimus, expressing that a most miserable but unknown man reposes below. The most heedless visitor is arrested by this sad voice speaking, as it were, from the ground ; and it is no wonder that the imaginations of poets and romancists have been awakened by it.

> " Miserrimus ! " and neither name nor date,
> Prayer, text, or symbol, graven upon the stone ;
> Nought but that word assigned to the unknown,
> That solitary word—to separate
> From all, and cast a cloud around the fate
> Of him who lies beneath. Most wretched one !
> *Who* chose his epitaph ?—Himself alone
> Could thus have dared the grave to agitate,
> And claim among the dead this awful crown ;
> Nor doubt that he marked also for his own,
> Close to these cloistral steps, a burial-place,
> That every foot might fall with heavier tread,
> Trampling upon his vileness. Stranger, pass
> Softly ! To save the contrite Jesus bled !

There has, of course, been much speculation regarding the identity of Miserrimus ; even a novel has been written upon the idea, containing striking events and situations, and replete with pathos. It is alleged, however, that the actual person was no hero, of strikingly unhappy story, but only a Rev. Thomas Morris, who, at the Revolution refusing to acknowledge the King's supremacy (more probably refusing to take the oaths to the new monarch), was deprived of his preferment, and depended for the remainder of his life on the benevolence of different Jacobites. At his death, viewing merely, we suppose, the extreme indigence to which he was reduced, and the humiliating way in which he got his living, he ordered that the only inscription on his tomb should be Miserrimus.

Such freaks are not unexampled, and we cannot be always sure that there is a real correspondence between the inscription and the fact. For instance, a Mr. Francis Cherry of Shottesbrooke, who died September 23, 1713, had his grave inscribed with no other words than Hic Jacet Peccatorum Maximus (Here lies the Chief of Sinners), the truth being, if we are to believe his friend Hearne, that he was an upright and amiable man, of the most unexceptionable religious practice—in Hearne's own words, " one of the most learned, modest, humble and virtuous persons that I ever had the honour to be acquainted with."

CHESTER CATHEDRAL.

William Smith, D.D. died 1787, aged 75.
As a scholar his reputation is perpetuated
by his valuable publications,
particularly his correct and elegant translations
of Longinus, Thucydides and Xenophon.
As a preacher he was admired, and
esteemed by his respective auditories :
And as a man, his memory remains inscribed
in the hearts of his friends.

Lowth, Bishop of London, died 1787.

If learning, genius, manners, void of guile,
The schoolman's labour, and the churchman's toil ;
If brightest parts, devoted but to good,
A soul which every selfish view withstood ;
If heavenly Charity's most winning charms,
And boundless Love, with ever-outstretched arms,
If all the tender and domestic train
Of private Virtues, such as grace the plain,
If God's viceregents, acting on that plan,
Which most endears man's dignity to man,
E'er won thy heart—Lowth's sacred shrine survey
And with a weeping world thy tearful tribute pay.

RICHMOND, SURREY.

In the earth, below this tablet
Are the remains of
James Thomson,
Author of the beautiful poems entitled,
The Seasons, Castle of Indolence, &c., &c.
Who died at Richmond on the 27th day of August
And was buried here on the 29th, old style, 1748.
The Earl of Buchan, unwilling that so good
A man
And sweet a poet should be without a memorial,
Has denoted the place of his interment,
For the satisfaction of his admirers,
In the year of our Lord, 1792.

" Father of light and life ! Thou good supreme !
O teach me what is good ! Teach me Thyself !
Save me from folly, vanity and vice,
From every low pursuit ! and feed my soul
With knowledge, conscious peace, and virtue pure,
Sacred, substantial, never fading bliss."

Thomson.

KIRKSTEAD, LANCS.

Near to this place lies interr'd
What was mortal of
John Taylor, D.D.
Reader,
Expect no Eulogium from this stone,
Enquire among the friends of
Learning, Liberty and Truth ;
These will do him justice.
Whilst taking his natural rest, he fell
Asleep in Jesus, the 5th of March, 1761
Aged 66.

St. Paul's Cathedral.

To the Memory of
Reginald Heber, D.D., Lord Bishop of Calcutta.
This Monument was erected by those who loved and
Admired him.
His character exhibited a rare union
of fervent zeal with universal tolerance,
Of brilliant talent with sober judgment,
And was especially distinguished by Christian humility,
Which no applause could disturb, no success abate.
He cheerfully resigned prospects of eminence at home
in order to become
The chief Missionary of Christianity in the East;
and having, in the short space of 3 years,
Visited the greater part of India,
and conciliated the affections and veneration
of men of every class of religion,
he was there summoned to receive the reward of
his labours, in the 43rd year of his age, 1826.

Thou art gone to the grave, but we will not deplore thee
Though sorrow and darkness encompass the tomb;
Thy Saviour has passed the portals before thee,
And the lamp of his love is thy guide through the gloom.

Thou art gone to the grave, but we will not deplore thee
Whose God was thy ransom, thy guardian and guide;
He gave thee, he took thee, and he will restore thee,
And Death has no sting, for the Saviour has died.

North Wrotham.

Samuel Wotton, D.D. died 1680.   Aged 80.

He learn'd to live, while he had breath
And so he lives even after Death.

Q

WENHASTON.

Sacred to the memory
Of the Rev. Thomas Leman, of Wenhaston-hall
in this parish
Who died on the 17th day of March, 1826,
the last male descendant of his ancient name.
He added to the feelings of a Gentleman
Talents and Learning without Ostentation,
And Christian Piety without Austerity.
In a curious line of antiquarian research
(the knowledge of Roman remains in Britain)
he had few superiors ;
but in the nobler and more amiable merit
of domestic life,
As a husband, a son, a brother, a friend and a master
he never was exceeded.
We flatter not in the grave !
" He that saw it bears record, and his record is true."
John xix, 25.
Bennet, Bishop of Cloyne.

WESTON FAVELL, NORTHANTS.

Rev. James Hervey.

Here lie the remains
of the Rev. James Hervey, A.M.
late rector of this parish ;
that very pious man,
And much admired author !
Who died Dec. 25, 1758
in the 45th year of his age.

Reader, expect no more ; to make him known,
Vain the fond elegy and figur'd stone ;
A name more lasting shall his writings give ;
There view display'd his heavenly soul and live !

ELTHAM.

Rev. George Horne, Bishop of Norwich.
Here lie interred
The earthly remains of
The Right Rev. George Horne, D.D.
Many years President of Magdalen College
in Oxford,
Dean of Canterbury
and late Bishop of Norwich.
In whose character
depth of learning, brightness of imagination,
Sanctity of manners and sweetness of temper,
Were united beyond the usual lot of mortality.
With his discourses from the pulpit,
his hearers, whether of the University,
the City, or the Country parish,
were edified and delighted.
His Commentary on the Psalms
will continue to be a companion to the closet
till the devotion of earth shall end
in the hallelujahs of heaven !
Having patiently suffered under such infirmities
as seemed not due to his years,
his soul took flight from this vale of misery,
to the unspeakable loss of the Church of England,
and his sorrowing friends and admirers,
Jan. 17th, 1792, in the 62nd year of his age.

REDENHALL.

Rev. John Rand, M.A.
His Wife and Daughter.

Three temples of the Holy Ghost,
Receiv'd by Death, ly here as lost,
St. John's fell first, St. Anne's next year,
Then St. Elizabeth fell here ;
Yet a few Dayes and thus againe,
Christ will rebuild in them reigne.

GLOUCESTER CATHEDRAL.

To the Memory of
William Warburton, D.D.
For more than six years bishop of this See.
A prelate
of the most sublime genius, and exquisite
Learning
Both which talents
He employed through a long life,
In the support
of what he firmly believed
The Christian Religion
And
of what he believed the best establishment
of it,
The Church of England.
He was born at Newark-upon-Trent
Dec. 24, 1698.
Died at his palace, in this City
June 7th, 1779.
And was buried near this place.

AT EXETER—1621.

On the Rev. William Cotton, D.D.
Bishop of Exeter.

Whom th' Queen from Paul to Peter did remove
Him God with Paul and Peter plac'd above.

1608.   Rev. Thos Playfere, D.D.

Who lives with Death, by Death in Death is lying,
But he who living dies, best lives by dying !
Who life to truth, who death to error gives,
In life may die, by death more surely lives.
My soul in Heaven breathes, in schools my fame,
Then on my tomb write nothing but my name.

FLINTSHIRE. 1776.

William Wynne, of Bower, D.D. aged 77.
Sometyme Fellow of All Souls College
in Oxford, and Rector of Llanvechan
in this diocese, departed this life
Aged (77)
In conformity to
Antient usage, from a proper
regard to decency, and a concern
for the health of his fellow creatures,
he was moved to give particular
directions for being buried in the
adjoining churchyard, and not in the
church ; and as he scorned flattering
of others while living, he has
took care to prevent being flattered
himself, when dead, by causing this
Small memorial to be set up
in his life time
God be merciful to me a sinner.

HAWKHURST.

Nathaniel Larder, D.D.
Drew his first and latest breath at Hall House, in this Parish.
Benevolent as a Gentleman,
Indefatigable as a Scholar,
exemplary as a Minister,
Wherever he resided.
His usefulness was prolonged to his 86th year ;
When
having established the Historical Credibility
of the Records of our common Salvation ;
without partiality, and beyond reply,
their promises became his eternal inheritance,
July 8, 1768
From reverence to the memory of his uncle
These truths were inscribed by David Jennings, 1789.

In the Church of Middleton Tyas.

This monument rescues from oblivion the remains of the Rev. John Mawer, D.D., late vicar of this parish, who died Nov. 18, 1763, aged sixty ; as also of Hannah Mawer, his wife, who died Dec. 22, 1766, aged seventy-two ; buried in the Chancel. They were persons of eminent worth. The Doctor was descended from the Royal family of Mawer, and was inferior to none of his illustrious ancestors in personal merit, being the greatest linguist this country ever produced. He was able to speak and write 22 languages, and particularly excelled in the Eastern tongues in which he proposed to His Royal Highness Frederick, Prince of Wales, to whom he was firmly attached, to propagate the Christian religion in the Abyssinian Empire ; a great and noble design, which was frustrated by the death of this excellent prince, to the great mortification of this excellent person, whose merit, meeting with no reward in this world, will, it is to be hoped, receive it in the next, from that Being which justice only can influence.

Rev. Dr. Trapp, died 1747.   Aged 75.

Death ! Judgment ! Heaven ! and Hell !

Think, Christians, Think !

You stand on vast Eternity's dread Brink.
Faith and Repentance, Piety and Prayer.
Despise *this* world, the *next* be all your care.
Thus while my Tomb the Solemn Silence breaks,
And to the eye this cold dumb marble speaks,
Tho' dead I preach, if e'er with ill Success,
Living, I strove th' important Truths to press,
Your precious, your immortal Souls to save,
Hear me, at least, O hear me from the Grave.

By Himself.

ALL SAINTS', WEST HADDON.

Rev. Griggory Palmer, died 1693.   Aged 85.

> Here lyeth honest Griggory,
> Which was a true friend to the Ministry ;
> And the soul's true friend for Eternity ;
> And one of the best fathers to his ability ;
> He studied the true form of Christianity,
> The which he hoped would abound to Posterity.

Rev. John Cotton, died 1652.

He was one of the early ministers of the Pilgrim Fathers' Community in New England. His epitaph was written by Mr. Woodbridge, and is supposed to have given the idea to Benjamin Franklin for his own epitaph.

> A living breathing bible ; tables where
> Both covenants at large engraven were :
> Gospel and law in heart had each its column,
> His head an index to the sacred volume.
> His very name a title page ; and next
> His life a commentary on the text.
> Oh ! What a monument of glorious worth,
> When in a new edition he comes forth
> Without errata, we may think he'll be
> In leaves and covers of Eternity.

HEREFORD CATHEDRAL.

Bishop Theophilus Field.
Anagram ! He failed not any.

> The Sun, that light unto three* Churches gave,
> Is set.   This Field is buried in a grave.
> This Sun shall rise, this Field renew his flowers,
> This sweetness breathe for ages, not for hours.

* He was successively Bishop of Llandaff, St. David's and Hereford.

NORWICH.

> 1575. Archbishop Matthew Parker.

Matthew Parker lived soberlie and wise,
Learned by Studie and continuall Practise,
Loving, true, of Life uncontroll'd,
The *Court* did foster him both young and old,
Orderlie he dealt, the Right he did defend,
He lived unto God, to God he made his end.

ST. PAUL'S.

> 1594. Bishop Aylmer, aged 73.

Eighteen years bishop, and once banished hence,
And twice a Champion in the truth's defence.

FULHAM.

In this vault is deposited the body of
The Right Reverend Father in God
Dr. Thomas Sherlock, late Bishop of this Diocese,
formerly Master of the Temple, Dean of Chichester,
and Bishop of Bangor and Salisbury.
whose beneficent and worthy conduct
in the several high stations which he filled,
entitled him to the gratitude of multitudes,
and the veneration of all.
His superior genius
his extensive and well applied learning,
his admirable faculty and unequalled power of reasoning,
as exerted in the explanation of Scripture,
in exhortations to that piety and virtue
of which he was himself a great example,
and in defence especially of Revealed Religion,
need no encomium here.
They do honour to the Age in which he lived ; and
will be known to posterity, without the help
of this perishable monument of stone.
Rev. Thomas Sherlock, D.D., died 1761. Aged 84.

Rev. Samuel Harvey, died 1729.   Aged 30.

Here lie the ruins of a lowly tent
Where the seraphic soul of Harvey spent
Its mortal years.   How did his genius shine,
Like Heaven's bright envoy, clad in powers divine !
When from his lips the grace and vengeance broke,
'Twas majesty in arms, 'twas melting mercy spoke.
What worlds of worth lay crowded in that breast !
Too straight the mansion for th' illustrious guest.
Zeal like a flame shot from the realms of day,
Aids the slow fever to consume the clay,
And bears the Saint up through the starry road
Triumphant !   So Elijah went to God.
What happy prophet shall this mantle find,
Heir to the double portion of his mind ?

Watts.

Wimple Church, Oxford.

A shining Starre that glistened farr when fix'd in this our
skye.
A radiant light shew'd to our sight of knowledge from on
hye
And by his Motion gave direction how wee should move on
earth
His influence store of Almes the poore in need received and
dearth
By many prayers and shower'ng teares this place his influence
had
Of comfort much and blessing such as joyed and made it
glad
This Starre so bright has lost its light being fallen to the
ground
His earth we have within this grave, his Soul in Heaven is
crown'd.

1625.   *Rev. Edward Marshall.   Aged 63.*

CHRIST CHURCH, OXFORD.

Robert Burton, author of the Anatomy of Melancholy.

Known to few, unknown to fewer, here lies Democritus junior, who lived and died by Melancholy. He died the 8th of the Ides of January, 1639.

INSTOW.

Here lie the ashes of that lamp divine
Which here with zeal did burn, with knowledge shine,
Such beams his life, and learning, did display,
As chang'd our twilight to a perfect day.
For which great light, this orb too low by far.
He's plac'd in heaven, and there shines as a star.

1631.   *Rev. John Down, B.D.*

Rev. John Donne, D.D.   Died 1631.

He that would write an epitaph for thee,
And write it well, must first begin to be
Such as thou wert; for none can truly know
Thy life and worth, but he that hath liv'd so.
He must have wit to spare and to hurl down,
Enough to keep the gallants of the town.
He must have learning plenty, both the laws
Civil and common, to judge any cause.
Divinity great store above the rest,
Not of the last edition, but the best.
He must have language, travel, all the arts,
Judgment to use, or else he wants thy parts.
He must have friends the highest, able to do,
Such as Mæcenas, and Augustus too,
He must have such a sickness, such a death
Or else his vain descriptions come beneath,
    He that would write an epitaph for thee
    Should first be dead: let it alone for me.

Bishop Corbet.

Bishopsbourne.

> Though nothing can be spoke worthy his fame,
> Or the remembrance of that precious name,
> Judicious Hooker ! though this cost be spent
> On him that hath a lasting monument
> In his own books ; yet ought we to express,
> If not his worth, yet our respectfulness.
> Church-ceremonies he maintained ; then why
> Without all ceremony should he die ?
> Was it because his life and death should be
> Both equal patterns of humility ?
> Or that perhaps, this only glorious one
> Was above all to ask, Why had he none ?
> Yet he that lay so long obscurely low
> Doth now, preferr'd, to greater honours go.
> Ambitious men learn hence to be more wise ;
> Humility is the true way to rise :
> And God in me this lesson did inspire,
> To bid this humble man, Friend, sit up higher.
>
> *W. Cooper.*
>
> 1600.   *Richard Hooker.*   *Aged* 46.

Beechy Island.

In memory of
Lieut. Bellot,
of the French Navy,
who lost his life whilst nobly
aiding in the search for
Sir John Franklin
In the Wellington Channel,
Where he was drowned
On the 18th of August, 1853.
This Tablet to record the sad event
was erected by a Friend,
A.D. 1854.

SAFFRON WALDEN.

Hon. H. A. and Grey Neville.

Sacred to the memory of two gallant young officers, the third and fifth sons of Lord and Lady Braybrooke, who, having accompanied their regiments to the Crimea, were both cut off in the short space of one week, while nobly fighting for their Queen and Country. The Hon. Henry Aldworth Neville, Captain in the Grenadier Guards, after sharing in the glories of the memorable day at Alma, was mortally wounded at the battle of Inkermann, Nov. 5, 1854, and expired a few hours after ; aged thirty.

The Hon. Grey Neville, Cornet in the 5th Dragoon Guards, died in the hospital at Scutari, Nov. 11th, 1854, of wounds received in the charge of the heavy cavalry at Balaclava, Oct. 25th, aged twenty-four.

"In the sight of the unwise they seemed to die, and their departure is taken for misery, and their going from us to be utter destruction, but they are in peace." Wisdom III, 2, 3.

GRANTHAM.

William Cust, R.N.
(Killed in the Expedition against Port Lewis, March 8, 1747).

He was in every relation of private life,
In all that concerned his Country, truly great,
And completed his course of life and glory
in the 28th year of his age.

Reader, thy life, how blest soe'er it be
Is but a voyage on a dangerous sea.
Would'st thou securely make the port of bliss,
See this brave youth, be thy great aim like his.
To live by general love, by virtue's laws,
Or die with honour in thy Country's cause.

IN HOLY TRINITY CHURCH, WINDSOR.

Monument to the Guards who fell at Alma and Inkermann.

To the memory of
Those gallant men,
The Officers,
Non-commissioned officers
and private soldiers
of the Brigade of Guards
who fell at
Alma and Inkermann,
And to those, who, no less brave,
have endured with unshaken fortitude,
even unto death
The dangers, severities and privations
of a Winter Campaign
before Sebastopol,
This Tablet is erected by
The Clergy of this Church
who ; in more peaceful times,
Ministered among them.
Easter, MDCCCLV.

SHRIVENHAM.

Here rests the Hero, who, in glory's page
Wrote his fair deeds for more than half an age.
Here rests the Patriot, who for England's good,
Each toil encountered, and each clime withstood ;
Here rests the Christian, his the loftier theme,
To seize the conquest, yet renounce the fame.
He, when his arm St. Lucia's trophies boasts,
Ascribes the glory to the Lord of Hosts ;
And when the harder task remain'd behind
The passive courage and the will resigned,
Patient the veteran victor yields his breath,
Secure in him who conquered sin and death.

Hannah More.

STONEHAM.

Admiral Lord Edward Hawke, died 1781. Aged 76.

The bravery of his soul was equal to the dangers he encountered ; the cautious intrepidity of his deliberations, superior even to the conquest he obtained ; the annals of his life compose a period of naval glory, unparalleled in later times, for wherever he sailed victory attended him ; a prince, unsolicited, conferred on him dignities he disdained to ask.

Charles, Marquis of Rockingham. Died 1782.

A statesman in whom constancy, fidelity, sincerity, and directness, were the sole instruments of his policy. His virtues were his arts. A clear, sound, unadulterated sense, not perplexed with intricate design, or disturbed by ungoverned passion, gave consistency, dignity, and effect to all his measures. In Opposition, he respected the principles of Government ; in Administration, he provided for the liberties of the people. He employed his moments of power in realising every thing which he had promised in a popular situation. This was the distinguishing mark of his conduct. After twenty-four years of service to the public, in a critical and trying time, he left no debt of just expectation unsatisfied.

By his prudence and patience he brought together a party which it was the great object of his labours to render permanent, not as an instrument of ambition, but as a living depository of principle.

The virtues of his public and private life, were not in him of different characters. It was the same feeling, benevolent, liberal mind that, in the internal relations of life, conciliates the unfeigned love of those who see men as they are, which made him an inflexible patriot. He was devoted to the cause of liberty, not because he was haughty and intractable, but because he was beneficent and humane.

Let his successors, who from this house behold his monument, reflect that their conduct will make it their glory or their reproach, let them be persuaded that similarity of manners, not proximity of blood, gives them an interest in this statue.

Remember—Resemble—Persevere.

E. Burke.

GREENWICH.

To the intrepid young
Bellot
of the French Navy
who in the endeavour to rescue
Franklin,
Shared the fate and glory of that
illustrious navigator.
(From his British Admirers)
1853.

NUNEHAM.

Frances Poole, Viscountess Palmerston, died 1769.

Here shall our ling'ring footsteps oft be found ;
This is her shrine, and consecrates the ground.
Here living sweets around hereafter rise,
And breathe perpetual incense to the skies.
Here too the thoughtless and the young may tread,
Who shun the drearier mansions of the dead ;
May here be taught what worth the world has known ;
Her wit, her sense, her virtue were her own ;
To her peculiar—and for ever lost
To those who knew, and therefore lov'd her most.
O, if kind Pity steal on Virtue's eye,
Check not the tear, nor stop the useful sigh ;
From soft Humanity's ingenuous flame,
A wish may rise to emulate her fame ;
And some faint image of her worth restore,
When those who now lament her are no more.

Whitehead.

Hamilton.

> James George, Seventh Duke of Hamilton.
> Died 1769. Aged 14.

All the reflected dignity that shines
Through the long annals of two princely lines,
And all that liberal nature could impart
To charm the eye and captivate the heart,
A bosom glowing with fair honour's flame,
A thirst for science and a love of fame,
With every genuine mark that could presage
Intrinsic greatness in maturer age,
Adorn'd the youthful tenant of this tomb,
Torn from his country's hopes in vernal bloom.
Whoe'er thou art that view'st this plaintive stone,
If e'er thy soul exulted o'er a son,
If public fame, avowing his desert,
Echoed the praises of thy partial heart,
Tho' all may mourn, 'tis thou alone must know
The piercing anguish of a parent's woe.

Moore.

In addition to the monument to John Hampden in Great Hampden, and which is given under the heading of Ancient Epitaphs, there is another, erected in 1843, on Chalgrove Field, by Lord Nugent.

Here in this field of Chalgrove, John Hampden, after an able and strenuous, but unsuccessful resistance in Parliament, and before the judges of the land, to the measures of an arbitrary court, first took arms, assembling the levies of the associated counties of Buckingham and Oxford, in 1642. And here, within a few paces of this spot, he received the wound of which he died, while fighting in the defence of the free monarchy and ancient liberties of England, June 18th, 1643. In the two hundredth year from that day, this stone was raised in reverence to his memory.